I0420042

CHINA'S RISE: THE STRATEGIC IMPACT OF ITS ECONOMIC AND MILITARY GROWTH

HEARING

BEFORE THE

SUBCOMMITTEE ON ASIA AND THE PACIFIC

OF THE

COMMITTEE ON FOREIGN AFFAIRS
HOUSE OF REPRESENTATIVES

ONE HUNDRED FOURTEENTH CONGRESS

FIRST SESSION

JUNE 17, 2015

Serial No. 114–72

Printed for the use of the Committee on Foreign Affairs

Available via the World Wide Web: http://www.foreignaffairs.house.gov/ or
http://www.gpo.gov/fdsys/

U.S. GOVERNMENT PUBLISHING OFFICE

95–128PDF   WASHINGTON : 2015

For sale by the Superintendent of Documents, U.S. Government Publishing Office
Internet: bookstore.gpo.gov   Phone: toll free (866) 512–1800; DC area (202) 512–1800
Fax: (202) 512–2104   Mail: Stop IDCC, Washington, DC 20402–0001

CONTENTS

CHINA'S RISE: THE STRATEGIC IMPACT OF ITS ECONOMIC AND MILITARY GROWTH

_____

WEDNESDAY, JUNE 17, 2015

House of Representatives,
Subcommittee on Asia and the Pacific,
Committee on Foreign Affairs,
Washington, DC.

The subcommittee met, pursuant to notice, at 1:06 a.m., in room 2255, Rayburn House Office Building, Hon. Matt Salmon (chairman of the subcommittee) presiding.

Mr. SALMON. The subcommittee will come to order. Let me start by recognizing myself and the ranking member to present our opening statements. Without objection, the members of the subcommittee can present brief remarks if they choose to or they can submit them for the record.

And now I am going to yield myself as much time as I may consume to present my opening remarks.

We can hardly discuss any major foreign policy issue without China coming up. Indeed, questions about China are on the top of everyone's minds. How stable is the Communist Party regime? How does China's land reclamation in the South China Sea affect prospects for peace or conflict? How can we deter China from hacking into our networks and stealing vital national security and economic information? Does China's activity reflect its growing global ambition or is it driven by domestic concerns for stability and security? What are the consequences of a slowdown of the Chinese economic machine on the U.S. economy?

China is at a crossroads. Its quest for development and global influence has come at a high cost of alienating partners and allies alike. There are cracks in the foundation, and imbalances remain politically, economically, and militarily. China cannot forsake and undermine the same international order that has helped incubate its rise to prominence. It cannot forget the agreements that it should honor or the spirit in which they were made.

I look forward to discussing these issues as I welcome our distinguished witnesses who traveled from as far as New York and Hong Kong to be here today.

China has become a global economic powerhouse since it opened up in 1978. China's military operation and expenditures, vast manufacturing, as well as regional investment and global infrastructure projects reflect this well. But the IMF projects China's annual GDP growth to slow down to about 5.9 percent over the next 6 years. Experts attribute the slowdown to factors such as demographic changes, the coddling of state-owned enterprises, a weak banking system, government corruption, and inadequate adherence to the rule of law.

Major demographic challenges are forcing changes to China's long-term economic planning, including the legacy of its one-child policy and increasing wealth gaps. The working class is simultaneously shrinking and demanding higher wages. Large debt loads throughout municipalities and provinces across the country mean that reckless infrastructure buildup is no longer viable for boosting GDP growth. The instruments that China used to finance its rise are no longer a reliable option for maintaining its position as a great economic power.

Innovation and access to information are major contributors to economic growth, but these drivers have been stifled because of China's desire to control information to protect domestic stability, leaving China in a development dilemma. These issues cannot be addressed when people cannot express ideas freely and benefit from their hard work. China can only throw so much money to try to foster intangible skills that contribute to an innovation society.

Instead, China resorts to stealing other nations' intellectual property, blatantly disregarding international norms, while stubbornly denying any malicious activity in cyberspace. Domestic drivers are protecting the governing power of the Chinese Communist Party. Continued economic growth and military modernization override its desire to curtail or halt such activity.

China's cyber activity cannot persist without repercussions. Yet, the high payoff for this behavior, and frankly, our inability to devise proper responses, exacerbate the issue.

Over the past 25 years, China has made great strides in military modernization, including a sustained 9.5 percent annual increase in military spending over the past decade. While it lacks combat experience and power projection capabilities, the People's Liberation Army attempts to address these shortcomings by conducting more noncombat operation overseas, participating in more international exercises, notably with Russia, and enhancing its ability to dominate territory in or around its waters. China's island-building activities contradict decades of international agreements in this arena and raise concerns and questions over its supposed peaceful rise.

Under Xi Jinping's leadership, punishment and detention for the exercise of free speech and assembly has been increasing. The government not only strictly controls the Internet and limits people's political and social rights, it also pursues efforts to forcibly assimilate ethnic and religious minorities, such as the Uighurs in Xinjiang. Legislation such as the Foreign NGOs Administration Law also put at risk our NGOs' ability to operate in China.

Promotion of human rights and protection of personal freedoms should continue to be an important aspect of our China policy. Under Xi Jinping's leadership, the world has seen a China that is both more internally restrictive and more internationally assertive. His predecessor, Deng Xiaoping, encouraged a low profile for China on the world stage, saying, "tao guang yang hui." Under Xi Jinping, however, China has embraced a higher international profile, chang-

ing its foreign affairs slogan to ''striving for achievements'' or ''fen
fa you wei.''

I have had the privilege to travel to China more than 40 times,
and I have had the honor to get to know many thoughtful, inspir-
ing, innovative, and successful Chinese people. If I have learned
anything from my years of engagement with China, it is that there
is no one way to characterize a country that is so full of wonder
and full of contradictions, full of frustration, yet full of potential.

As the United States prepares for Xi Jinping's visit on September
1, I urge our Government to welcome China's active role in the
world, but we must also temper China's impatience and assertive-
ness with expectations of reciprocity and responsibility.

I now recognize the ranking member, Brad Sherman, for his remarks.

Mr. SHERMAN. Thank you, Mr. Chairman. We are, of course,
holding these hearings an hour early. I got about 1½ hours' notice
of that. So let the record show that I was not 2 minutes late to
these hearings. I was 58 minutes early.

Mr. SALMON. Right.

Mr. SHERMAN. And I would hope that members who wish to give
short opening statements be allowed to do so whenever they are
able to arrive.

We have two great issues with China, economic and geopolitical.
It is my observation that in our country, whenever we are making
a decision, we tend to make it in lines with the institutional needs
of the most powerful institution that cares about that policy. So in
the area of military affairs, we tend to make decisions meeting the
institutional needs of the Pentagon. In the area of economics, we
tend to make decisions based upon the institutional needs of Wall
Street and the corporate sector.

And with regard to China, this has led to a bizarre schizophrenia
where we are about to fight China for islets that are useless and
not ours and make every possible concession on trade, while never
talking about using trade to tell China they better not take islands
if we care about the islands, which I am not sure we should. Islets,
I might add.

Look at the Pentagon as an institution. Every time since 1898
when we have faced a uniformed nation-state as an adversary it
has been a glorious outcome for our military forces, none more glorious than the defeat of the Soviet Union, which basically took
place by facing them down rather than engaging in kinetic warfare.
Every time since 1898 that we have faced an asymmetrical oppo-
nent, every time we have faced a nonuniformed adversary, it has
been very painful for our Pentagon and military forces. We have
not always lost, but since the Philippine insurrection, it has always
been painful.

So the Pentagon, if it is going to meet its institutional needs,
needs to find a worthy adversary. There is only one, and that is
China. And that is why every decision at the Pentagon is how can
we ignore the Middle East and reconfigure our forces to pivot toward a confrontation with the People's Republic of China. Every
decision as to what research to do, every decision as to how to pro-
cure, force configuration, it is all about how can we fight the war—

or the face-off, hopefully, not a kinetic war—that will meet our institutional needs.

China does not have to be the enemy, but it is the only enemy that meets the Pentagon's institutional needs. Keep in mind when it comes to these islets, there is no oil, they are worthless. If they are standing astride trade routes, those are trade routes in and out of Chinese ports. If China controls them, they will have the geopolitical, strategic capacity to blockade their own ports, but they do not stand in a position to interfere with U.S. trade with Japan, the Philippines, et cetera.

And there is no oil. If there was any oil, it wouldn't be our oil. And Japan, for example, spends almost nothing of its GDP to defend the islets that don't have any oil, but if it was oil, it would be Japanese oil.

And China is part of this. They are meeting their institutional needs by whipping up nationalism over useless islets.

When it comes to trade, the trade deal that is before Congress now is the most incredible gift to China and the most incredible gift to Wall Street. China is not a party, so they have no cost, no commitments. They don't have to pay a penny for this deal. But what do they get?

First, a declaration by the world that the trade agreements of the 21st century will allow, even encourage currency manipulation, which of course is their number one way of taking American jobs.

Second, the rules of origin provision. Goods can be made, admittedly, 60 percent made in China, but that really means 80 percent made in China in reality, finished in Japan, finished in Vietnam, and get fast tracked into the American market. So it is 80 percent of all the benefits of signing a free trade agreement with the United States and zero percent of the cost.

I would point out that while we run a $300 billion trade deficit with China, Germany has a balanced trade relationship with China. If we had a balanced trade relationship with China there would be a labor shortage in this country. Companies would be desperate to hire more people, they would be raising wages, they would be hiring the barely unqualified and then training them. A higher percentage of GDP would be going to labor. Wall Street does not want that. And this agreement ensures that we will continue to have the wage stagnation, or from the other side, labor cost non-increase that Wall Street would like to see.

Finally, we have one tactic that we could be using against China and probably should, and that is, gather the information—they are hacking us all the time—gather the information that proves that their top 1,000 cadres are corrupt and expose that information, as is appropriate, whether it be those who are the insiders like or those who are on the outs, whether it be those who are popular locally, those who are not popular locally, whether it be that we demand concessions, otherwise we will expose, or whether we actually expose in order to undermine the regime's image that it is fighting for the Chinese people.

Of course, we are reluctant to do that, just as we are reluctant to have any of the hundreds of tax cheats in our own country who are exposed in multimillion-dollar revelations from banks subject to our criminal law, but we need to have dossiers on the economic corruption of the top 1,000 Chinese officials.

And I yield back.

Mr. SALMON. Thank you.

Let me just make a comment on the timing of the hearing. There really wasn't anything sinister afloat. They changed the votes to 3 o'clock today, which would have given us time for a 15-minute hearing, which didn't do justice when we have got somebody that came all the way from Hong Kong to meet with us.

So we apologize for the changes to the people testifying today and to members of the committee. We did the best we could today with a very difficult situation.

I recognize Mr. Duncan.

Mr. DUNCAN. I thank the chairman and apologize. I will have to leave, due to the schedule change, at 1:30.

I think it is prudent that we remind ourselves of Proverbs 22:7, which says the borrower is servant to the lender. China's actions in the Spratlys and the South China Sea are inexcusable, and what should the U.S. do about it, given that China is such a strong economic power? And what should the U.S. do about that? Definitely not unilaterally, but also possibly working with the Philippines that are dramatically affected with the incursion in the Spratlys that we see.

China's posturing is alarming. China is attempting to reshape international economics as well as geopolitics. And one thing that concerns me that I hope this committee will delve into is China's, for lack of any word, gobbling up mineral rights around the globe, especially when it comes to rare earth minerals, which they understand and we fail to recognize enough that they are vital to the technical systems of today, such as your iPhone, your iPad, and all the technology that really drives our economy.

So these are some things that I hope we delve into, and I appreciate the chairman for having this hearing. And I yield back.

Mr. SALMON. Thank you.

Mr. DesJarlais, did you have any opening comments?

Mr. Perry.

Mr. PERRY. Sure. Thank you, Mr. Chairman.

The U.S.-China relationship is entering a new phase. Beijing has become more confident, global, and assertive. In a relationship that has unique cooperative and competitive elements, no one, none will stress a relationship more than those concerning the South China Sea. American efforts to protect our interests against this newly aggressive China have been, in my opinion, ineffective. In official public statements, the Obama administration takes no position on the disputed formal territorial claims and then calls for peaceful resolution of disputes.

American objectives for the South China Sea must be a part of a larger strategy toward China that welcomes a greater Chinese economic and diplomatic role. It can't just be rhetoric and talk about a pivot without any action. We must set clear boundaries on Chinese expansion of its territory by coercion or conquest, and on its ability to deny the United States full freedom of action in the Western Pacific.

And with that, Mr. Chairman, I yield back.

Mr. SALMON. Thank you.

Now we get to the panel. Pursuant to Committee Rule 7, the members of the subcommittee will be permitted to submit written statements to be included in the official hearing record. Without objection, the hearing record will remain open for 7 days to allow statements, questions, and extraneous materials for the record subject to length limitation in the rules.

Okay. We are honored today to have the distinguished panel before the subcommittee. Dr. Derek Scissors is a resident scholar at the American Enterprise Institute where he focuses on Asian economic issues. One of Dr. Scissors' areas of specialty is the economy of China and Chinese-U.S. economic relations.

Dr. Alison Kaufman is a senior research scientist at the CNA Corporation's China Strategic Issues Group. One of her areas of expertise is U.S. security cooperation in the region.

Thank you for being here.

Jerome Cohen is currently a professor of law at New York University School of Law as well as the co-director of the U.S.-Asia Law Institute. Mr. Cohen has practiced law and lived in China for decades, since before the country opened up to the world.

Mr. Dongfang Han is currently the executive director of the China Labour Bulletin. Mr. Han helped to form China's first independent trade union in 1989, and in the aftermath of the crackdown following the Tiananmen Square protests, he was arrested and detained for nearly 2 years. He has led a long career as a voice for reform and rights in China.

I really enjoyed my meeting in Hong Kong with you, and I am so excited about you being here today.

Adam Hersh is a senior economist at the Roosevelt Institute and a visiting fellow at Columbia University's Institute for Policy Dialogue. Previously he was a senior economist at the Center for American Progress.

And without objection, the record will remain open for 5 business days during which members may submit materials for the permanent record.

And you all understand the lighting system. You have 5 minutes to speak. I don't do a heavy gavel. If you have a few seconds over, no problem. But the light turns amber when you have got about a minute left. Just be cognizant of that. When it turns red, it is like my wife tells me when I am speaking, it is time for this.

So I appreciate you being here today. We are extremely happy to have you here. I am going to start on the left side of the dais with—my left, your right—Dr. Scissors.

STATEMENT OF DEREK M. SCISSORS, PH.D., RESIDENT SCHOLAR, AMERICAN ENTERPRISE INSTITUTE

Mr. SCISSORS. Thank you, Mr. Chairman, and thank you to the committee for inviting me here.

I am going to start by saying that the chairman's remarks about the great variety in China apply to U.S. studies of China as well. There are other research communities represented here who have very different perspectives for very good reasons.

From my perspective—and I title my written testimony not "China's Rise" but "China's Stall"—so the econperspective on China is quite different than perhaps the national security or the human rights perspective.

To summarize it, the China stall is not unavoidable, but the problem is more than a decade old at this point. The government is going to report whatever it wants, the Chinese Government can report whatever economic statistics it likes, but by the end of this decade it will be unmistakable that China is no longer growing economically, unless significant market reforms are resumed.

That is the theme of my presentation. It has a lot of implications, which hopefully we will get to in the rest of the hearing.

Let me give some qualifiers. I am not saying China is about to collapse. That is a different argument. I think it is unjustified. China's economic situation of high debt and aging population—and you see a picture up on the board—inadequate local innovation, that is not a collapse situation. That is a stagnation situation. So people talking about collapse are saying different things than I am saying here.

I do think, rather, that China can avoid this, can have another generation of rapid growth, which would be very impressive on the top of the one it has already had, but it has to go back to what got it there in the first place, which is—should I yield my time to Congressman Rohrabacher?

Mr. SALMON. Go ahead.

Mr. SCISSORS. Okay. It has to go back to what got it there in the first place, which is individual property rights and competitive markets.

And my third caveat would be is I don't really care about GDP. I certainly don't care about Chinese GDP. The Chinese Government doesn't tell the truth about their GDP growth. I don't think GDP is a very good measure. What matters, especially in mixed command-market economies, is how well you are delivering the goods to households. So what I care about when I am saying China is stagnating, I am not talking about what they are going to report in 2020. I am talking about household and personal income growth.

Okay. So how am I saying this? The problems go back to 2003. In that year the then new government under Hu Jintao pushes aside market reform in favor of public investment, directed and financed by the state, largely routed through state-owned enterprises. 2003 to 2008, China's economy is getting bigger and it is getting less healthy. The equivalent of my wife's comment is: At 190 pounds, you were fine, you didn't get stronger when you added the extra 20 pounds. She says that, I don't know, once in a while, this morning, yesterday, you name it. That is what was going on in China 2003 to 2008.

You didn't see that when the numbers were soaring, but when the financial crisis hit, China's vulnerability was much higher. They were much more vulnerable to a drop in excess demand, they were much more leveraged. They actually got structurally weaker in those 5 years even though they got bigger.

Then they had a horrible crisis response, which is to order their banks, because they control the banks, to lend to everyone, without discrimination, when no one could make money. So you would think that the United States would be the champion of debt problems. The financial crisis starts here. We had private sector debt problems. We brought a lot of the private sector debt into the public sector. China's debt problems since 2008 are much worse than ours, not even close. And I could give you some numbers, but I want to get to my implications of this.

So what is the forecast for China's growth? When you have high debt and you have overspent, you don't have a return on capital. You have already wasted a ton of money, you have to use a lot of your money to pay back debt, that is not going to drive growth. Aging, public health problems, labor, which has been a big contributor to Chinese growth, is not going to drive growth. Environmental destruction, which means the land, which was the original driver of Chinese growth in the late 1970s and early 1980s, not going to drive growth.

Innovation, which both the chairman and the ranking member, several members have talked about, it is a very rough transition to go from copying and stealing other people's technology to developing your own, and what China needs to push growth higher is to develop its own technology, but that can't be ordered the way espionage programs can be ordered. So that is not a clear source of growth either. In fact, I think it is much more likely we are going to be dealing with China stealing U.S. technology and information than we are China driving innovation.

Sources of growth are pretty easy. China is going to stagnate. And the way to get away from that is reform, which they have talked about, but it requires fewer restrictions on labor mobility so people can go where the jobs are. That makes the Ministry of Public Security very uncomfortable. My colleague may discuss this. I don't mean to put any words in his mouth.

They need a competitive financial system instead of one run by the state. They need a smaller state sector so that the private sector can actually compete in more industries. They need private rural land rights. The state owns all rural land. Individuals can't own rural land.

So this is a very tall order, and they have a long, long way to go. And I have to be cynical here. I don't believe governments do things until they actually do them. IOUs don't cut it. So right now China is on a path to stagnation, not a path to reform.

I don't really have time for implications. There are a lot. I will say that the economic impact on the U.S. is not very large. We can talk more about that. I think there are some important strategic issues. I am not qualified to talk about some of them. One of them I am. Ranking Member Sherman said correctly: We should be spending more resources gathering information. I wrote a paper about this a couple of years ago. We can have differences over what information we want to gather. But we have a China that could stall. We were caught off guard when the Soviet Union's economy didn't work. We shouldn't have that happen again.

Thank you.

[The prepared statement of Mr. Scissors follows:]

China's Stall

Testimony submitted to the House Committee on Foreign Affairs, Subcommittee on Asia and the Pacific

in advance of the hearing "China's Rise"

June 17, 2015

By Derek Scissors

Resident Scholar, American Enterprise Institute

Note: the following represents the views of the author, only, not any organization-wide positions held by the American Enterprise Institute.

It is often forgotten that changes in economic policy can require years to make an impact. Recalling this is important in understanding China's economic trajectory. The most common description today is that China is slowing. In fact, it is stagnating.

In 1978, China began to grant limited private property rights and to permit limited competition. These steps helped create an economic miracle, among other things lifting 850 million people out of poverty over a generation. But for more than a decade now, the Communist Party has chosen not to move forward on private property rights and competition, instead emphasizing an unprecedented amount of state-directed spending. The result is a severely damaged environment, an unbalanced economy, and a painful debt burden.

This is not hindsight. The stagnation path was visible six years ago, when China choose to massively expand credit in response to the financial crisis. Weaknesses in the economy can be traced back to policies initiated six years before that, in 2003.[1] Because the fault lines have been developing for some time, they will require years of difficult reform to address. The current government has pledged such reform but largely lacked the nerve to initiate it, much less sustain it. The single most likely result is that China will share the fate of many other economies and fall far short of being wealthy.

Stagnation, Not Collapse

Stagnation does not translate to China becoming unimportant, and certainly not to a collapse. China bulls often criticize bears for predicting a crisis that never occurs.[2] As a long-time bear, I have never predicted an economic collapse. The reason: a mixed market-state economy is less vulnerable to an acute crisis and more vulnerable to chronic, serious problems. The Communist Party can control the economy and has overwhelming motivation to avoid a crisis. While an economic stall is hardly appealing, it is both less terrifying to the Party and harder to avoid.

As an illustration, China cannot have "a Lehman moment." Commercial financial systems like those in the West are only as strong as their weakest link. But Chinese finance is dominated by the state.[3] Non-commercial financial systems are as weak as their strongest link because the government can, without legal or political delay, order the strongest institutions to save the weakest. The cost, of course, is a financial system that wastes enormous sums of money.

---

[1] Derek M. Scissors, "China Refuses to Adjust Its Economy," Heritage Foundation, July 16, 2009, http://www.heritage.org/research/reports/2009/07/china-refuses-to-adjust-its-economy; Derek M. Scissors, "Deng Undone: The Costs of Halting Market Reform in China," *Foreign Affairs*, May/June 2009, https://www.foreignaffairs.com/articles/china/2009-05-01/deng-undone-0.

[2] Tom Orlik, "Crisis, What Crisis? How to Beat Back the China Bears." *Wall Street Journal*, February 24, 2012, http://blogs.wsj.com/chinarealtime/2012/02/24/crisis-what-crisis-how-to-beat-back-the-china-bears/

[3] Grant Turner, Nicholas Tan, and Dena Sadchian, *The Chinese Banking System* (Sydney: Reserve Bank of Australia, 2012), http://www.rba.gov.au/publications/bulletin/2012/sep/pdf/bu-0912-7.pdf; Derek M. Scissors, "Why China cannot have a 'Lehman moment'." *South China Morning Post*, February 24, 2014, http://www.scmp.com/business/banking-finance/article/1433983/why-china-cannot-have-lehman-moment.

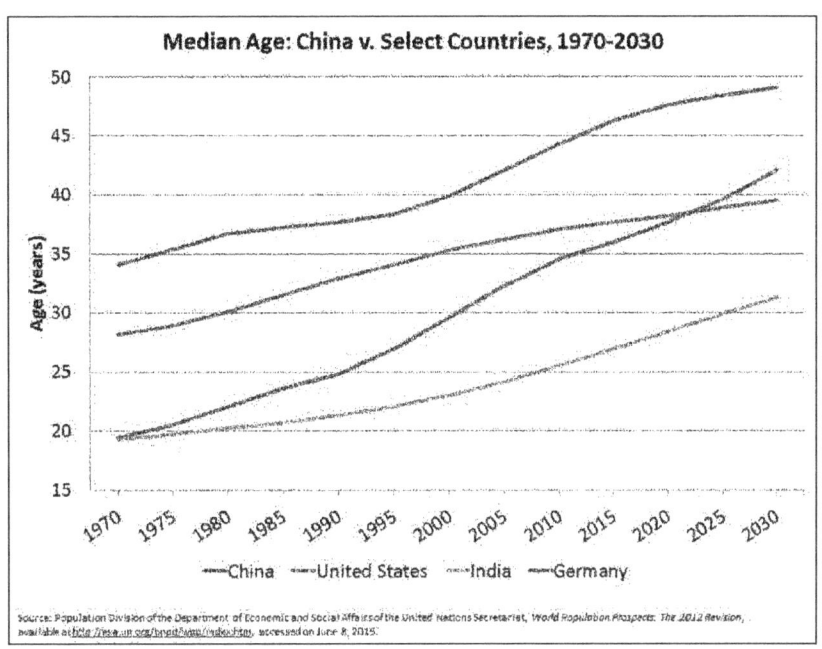

Median Age: China v. Select Countries, 1970-2030

Source: Population Division of the Department of Economic and Social Affairs of the United Nations Secretariat, *World Population Prospects: The 2012 Revision*, available at http://esa.un.org/unpd/wpp/index.htm, accessed on June 8, 2015.

Demography also argues for stagnation and against collapse. Demography can cause social and political crisis when there are too many young people and not enough jobs. China is aging, instead, and the challenge for aging societies is not riots but stasis.[4]

It is certainly also the case that a stagnant China will remain be large and important. It will be one of the world's top manufacturers and traders, and perhaps the leader in absolute size in these areas. For spending overseas, it will still have several trillion dollars in official foreign exchange reserves plus another trillion in foreign exchange at state banks. At home, it will have huge asset and debt markets – especially for property but also for securities. China's growth is vanishing, its size and stability remain.

Climbing Everest

The first step in understanding why stagnation is likely is to consider other countries. While the categories can be fluid, far more economies rise out of poverty than become truly rich. This is sometimes referred to as the middle-income trap.[5]

---

[4] Anthony Kuhn, "One Country Provides Preview of China's Looming Aging Crisis," NPR, January 14, 2015. http://www.npr.org/sections/parallels/2015/01/14/377190697/one-county-provides-preview-of-chinas-looming-aging-crisis.

[5] Barry Eichengreen, Donghyun Park, and Kwanho Shin, "Growth Slowdowns Redux: New Evidence on the Middle-Income Trap" (working paper, National Bureau of Economic Research, Cambridge, MA, 2013).

In the post-war era, the most impressive economic success stories are in East Asia, which seems to bode well. However, Japan became rich by global standards before World War II and its burst of growth 1946-1990 was in large part regaining previously held ground. Hong Kong and Singapore are not even large cities by Chinese standards. Taiwan's total population is about the same as Shanghai's. Most of the rich oil exporters are also micro-states.

The only country with a population over 30 million that has become rich for the first time in the post-war era is South Korea. Meanwhile, the list of countries that have not gone beyond middle-income is long – Argentina, Indonesia, and Thailand, to name a few. It would not be unusual if there were cities in China with income levels similar to, say France. It would be highly unusual for China as a whole to reach French levels of income.

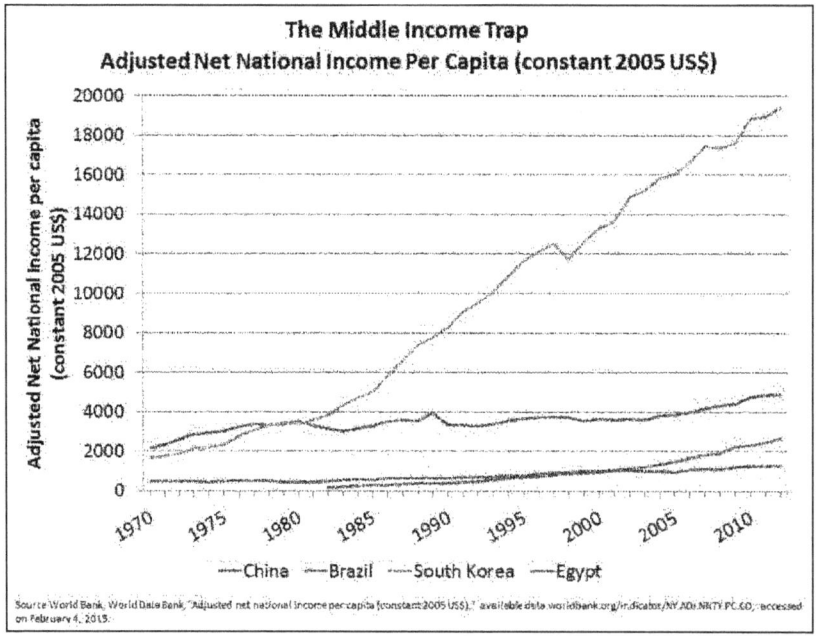

The second stop is to evaluate Chinese growth. The government continues to report comparatively rapid gains in gross domestic product (GDP) and most likely will do so indefinitely. But official statistics are not a reliable indicator of how the economy is doing. The statistics bureau opened its most recent communiqué as follows:[6]

---

[6] National Bureau of Statistics of China, "Statistical Communique of the People's Republic of China on the 2014 National Economic and Social Development," news release, February 26, 2015.

In 2014, faced with the complicated and volatile international environment and the heavy tasks to maintain the domestic development, reform and stability, the Central Party Committee and the State Council led the people of all nationalities of China to seize the momentum of international and domestic development, adhere to the general tone of "moving forward while maintaining stability", fully deepen the reform and opening up, focus on the innovation of macro control, tap into the vitality of the market and foster the driving force of innovation.

This is hardly reassuring as to the willingness of government statisticians to publish anything the Party does not like.

Just as important, GDP is wildly overrated as a measure of economic success.[7] For one thing, it makes no sense to use GDP per person, since no one can spend it. In terms of what people actually have in their pockets, China reported disposable income per person equivalent to $3360 at the end of 2014 (the US figure was $41,180). Plainly, there is a long way to go.

Already slowing would therefore be worrisome enough by itself for China's prospects. And slowing may understate the problem. Credit Suisse reports private wealth figures for all major economies.[8] From the end of 2011 to the middle of 2014 (latest available), China's net private wealth grew 10 percent, total. World wealth grew 17 percent; far from being world-leading, China underperformed.

Private wealth is volatile, and Chinese private wealth is likely rising now due to a skyrocketing stock market. Private wealth is also only part of the story, especially in China where the state owns so much in the way of assets. At the core of any notion of economic growth -- GDP, wealth, or others -- is productivity. Productivity is difficult to measure but it may be that Chinese productivity actually declined 2008-12.[9] If that is accurate, it is far more important than what the government claims GDP is.

With the Wrong Guide

Whether or not productivity did start to decline in 2008, China's economic problems have been brewing for quite a while. They did not begin this year or last, as some seem to think.[10] They did not even begin with the financial crisis. They began in 2003.

From 1978-2002, pro-market reform was partial and uneven, But it was persistent and it created an economic powerhouse. In 2003, a then-new government under Communist Party General Secretary Hu Jintao decided that state-owned banks lending to state-owned enterprises should lie

---

[7] Michael Pettis, "What multiple should we give China's GDP growth?" Michael Pettis' China Financial Markets, May 17, 2015. http://blog.mpettis.com/2015/05/what-multiple-should-we-give-chinas-gdp-growth/.

[8] *Global Wealth Databook 2014* (Credit Suisse Research Institute, 2014), https://publications.credit-suisse.com/tasks/render/file/?fileID=5521F296-D460-2B88-081889DB12817E02

[9] Harry X. Wu, "China's Growth and Productivity Performance Debate Revisited: Accounting for China's Sources of Growth with a New Data Set" (working paper, Conference Board China Center, Beijing, 2014).

[10] Andrew Ross Sorkin, "A Veteran of the Financial Crisis Tells China to Be Wary," *New York Times*, April 21, 2015, http://www.cnbc.com/id/102605452.

at the core of the economy, so that these badly-run firms could continue to employ large numbers of people and serve as economic tools for the Party.[11]

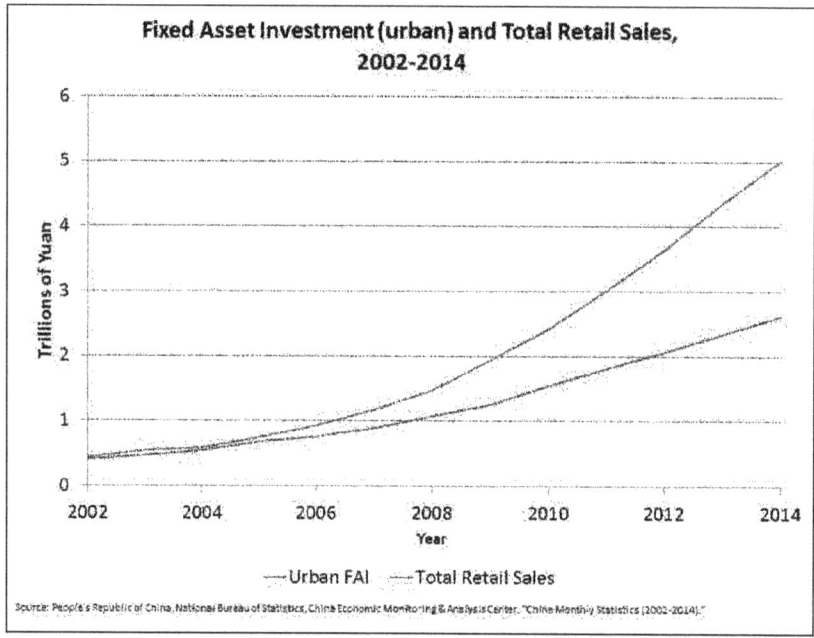

Market forces would still play an important role, but fresh market-oriented reforms would be limited, supplanted by ever-rising amounts of investment. Official investment growth jumped from 12 percent in 2001 past 26 percent in 2003, more than four-fifths by state-controlled enterprises. Investment growth then exceeded 25% annually for the next 9 years, doubling the pace of official GDP.[12] The dependence on investment and huge imbalance between investment and consumption was not always a feature of the economy, it was created by the Hu regime starting in late 2002.

And at first it seemed to work. Chinese companies borrowed, invested, produced, and exported, and growth soared. This was in no small part, however, a mirage. Behind the glitter was not the

---

[11] Hu Angang, Hu Linlin, and Chang Zhixiao, *China's economic growth and poverty reduction, 1978-2002* (New Delhi: International Monetary Fund, 2003); Deng Shasha, "Factbox: China's fixed assets investment booms over decade," Xinhua, August 23, 2012, http://news.xinhuanet.com/english/china/2012-08/23/c_131803358.htm.
[12] People's Republic of China, National Bureau of Statistics, China Economic Monitoring & Analysis Center. "China Monthly Statistics (2001-2011)."

greater productivity that arises from market reform but increasing dependence on domestic credit to finance investment and on foreign consumption to buy the goods ultimately produced. [13]

The global financial crisis therefore came as a double blow. First, foreign demand plummeted. Then, on top of the intervention through public investment starting in 2003, the Party conducted what was arguably history's biggest stimulus through bank loans. Bank credit grew 32 percent in 2009, even as profit opportunities disappeared. Credit expansion has slowed but remains staggering. In a smaller economy, China's broad money supply M_2 is now no less than 75% larger than America's. [14]

There are many people who urge the extension of enormous amounts of credit when demand falls. Using official numbers, however, China did not need to respond in such terror in 2009. Even assuming official numbers at the time were useless, the inevitable outcome of borrowing to avoid a downturn is too much capacity and growth-killing debt. In 2003, the government identified 3 industries as suffering overcapacity; in 2013, that number had ballooned to 19. [15]

It gets worse. China's debt may now be the world's largest, where the highest estimate has it closing on $30 trillion. Two-thirds of that has been accumulated in the past 8 years. There are two complementary and powerful consequences. First, when a country has already spent so much, the return on yet more spending is low. This is the main reason growth is slowing. Second, when a country's debt is so large, a good deal of capital is spent paying it back. [16] This is the main reason growth will slow further.

[13] Li Cui, "China's Growing External Dependence," *Finance and Development* 44, no. 3 (2007).

[14] Xiong Tong, "China reports record 9.59 trln yuan in loans in 2009," Xinhua, January 1, 2015, http://news.xinhuanet.com/english/2010-01/15/content_12816059.htm;
People's Republic of China, National Bureau of Statistics, China Economic Monitoring & Analysis Center, "China Monthly Statistics (2001-2011).": Board of Governors of the Federal Reserve System (US), *M2 Money Stock*. June 12, 2015, https://research.stlouisfed.org/fred2/series/M2/

[15] US-China Economic and Security Review Commission, *China's Role in the Origins of and Response to the Global Recession*, February 17, 2009 (statement of Nicholas R. Lardy, Peterson Institute of Economics).

[16] Richard Dobbs, Susan Lund, Jonathan Woetzel, and Mina Mutafchieva, *Debt and (not much) deleveraging* (McKinsey & Co., 2015); James Kynge. "China's real interest rate surges to post-crisis high," *Financial Times*, May 18, 2015, http://www.ft.com/intl/cms/s/0/74990c3c-fd69-11e4-b072-00144feabdc0.html#axzz3cbzlB1Jr.

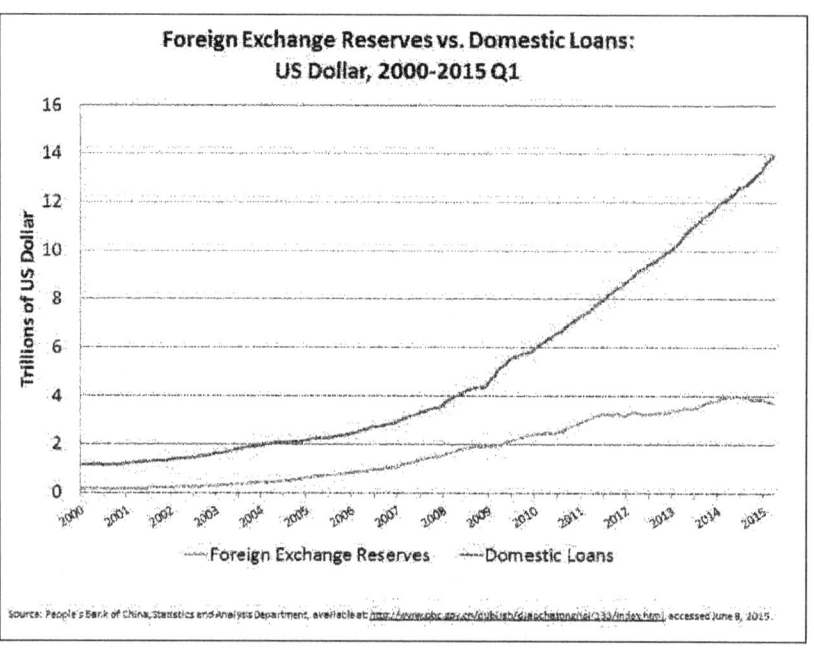

Foreign Exchange Reserves vs. Domestic Loans: US Dollar, 2000-2015 Q1

Source: People's Bank of China, Statistics and Analysis Department, available at http://www.pbc.gov.cn/publish/diaochatongjisi/133/index.html, accessed June 8, 2015.

There are other reasons. Best-known, China is moving rapidly from a young to an old country. The government says the number of working age people started to fall in 2012 and has fallen more sharply each year since. This may not be entirely accurate but it is certain that the work force will shrink during this decade and throughout the next. The contribution of labor to growth will fade until labor actually detracts from growth, as it does in Japan and parts of Europe. It is not inevitable, but old countries tend to stagnate economically.[17]

In addition, growth based on natural resources has disappeared. In the 1980's, farm productivity soared, permitting what were unnecessary farmers to become manufacturing workers and helping create the word's new factory. Land and natural resources will not spur economic growth again for the foreseeable future, as China has badly depleted its resource endowment.[18]

Illustrations of this range from arable land to zinc deposits, but perhaps the clearest is water. The World Bank cites water stress as occurring below 1000 meters^3 of water per person per year; northern China is at one-fifth that amount. Three-fifths of monitored groundwater sites are rated

---

[17] Laura Zhou, "China's workforce shrinks by nearly 4 million amid greying population," *South China Morning Post*, January 20, 2015, http://www.scmp.com/news/china/article/1683778/chinas-workforce-shrinks-nearly-4-million-amid-greying-population; Phil Coggan, "Secular stagnation," *Economist*. November 3. 2014, http://www.economist.com/blogs/buttonwood/2014/11/secular-stagnation.

[18] Zhun Xu, Wei Zhang, and Minqi Li, "China's Grain Production: A Decade of Consecutive Growth or Stagnation?" *Monthly Review* 66, no. 1 (2014); *Report on Ecological Footprint in China* (China Council for International Cooperation on Environment and Development and World Wildlife Fund, 2012).

by the central government as unfit for drinking.[19] Just as China will be forced to make hefty payments on its financial debt, it will be forced to on its environmental debt, also making economic growth more difficult.

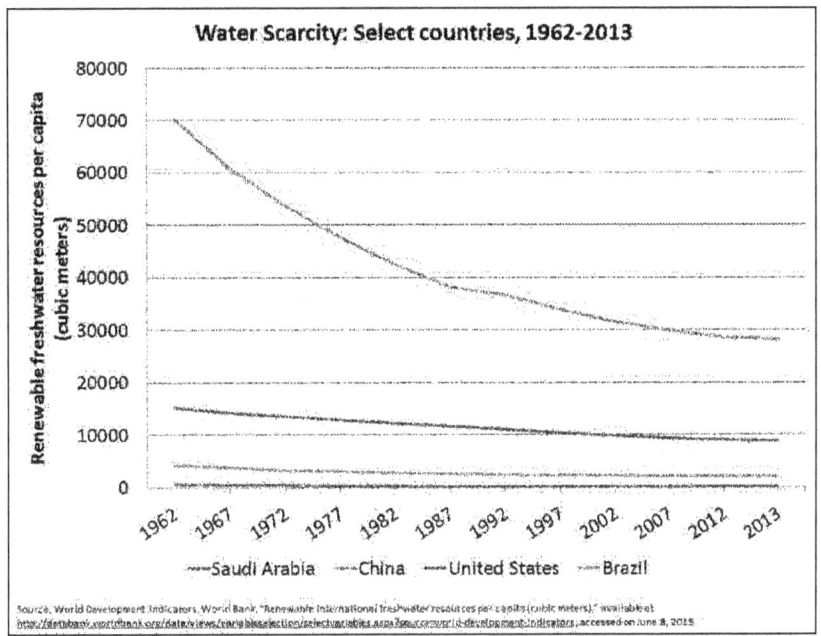

A final way to achieve growth is through innovation, which is the hardest category to measure. China has successfully imported foreign technology, legally and illegally (though theft of intellectual property).[20] As countries climb the technological ladder, however, they can no longer merely absorb what others offer. Fresh innovation becomes more challenging. Moreover, weakness in other sources of growth means that China must increasingly rely on innovation if the economy is to continue to expand.

The government recognizes all this but its strategy is exactly wrong. Sustained, broad innovation that drives growth must be bottom-up, but the somewhat infamous indigenous innovation

---

[19] "Rivers are disappearing in China. Building canals is not the solution," *Economist*, October 10, 2013, http://www.economist.com/news/leaders/21587789-desperate-measures; "Over 60% of underground water substandard: report," *China Daily*, April 24, 2014, http://www.chinadaily.com.cn/china/2015-04/24/content_20529263.htm.
[20] *The IP Commission Report* (Commission of the Theft of American Intellectual Property. National Bureau of Asian Research, 2013), http://www.ipcommission.org/report/ip_commission_report_052213.pdf.

program is top-down, as if the government can anticipate all the needed changes for years to come.[21] This is not how innovation occurs in computing, telecom, energy and elsewhere.

The policies that support innovation are also deeply flawed. Intellectual property even within China is not protected well, reducing the incentive to innovate. Continued regulatory protection of state-owned enterprises (SOEs) means the private sector is simply not allowed to succeed in the two dozen industries that SOEs dominate, which also reduces the incentive to innovate.[22] In innovation, as in capital, labor, and land, China must have profound reforms or it will stall.

Reform to the Rescue?

State intervention into the economy brought China to this point. More state action, such as interest rates cuts or yet more infrastructure spending, will not reverse it. Reversal requires a resumption of market reform. The Party claims to have recognized this under current General Secretary Xi Jinping. Its November 2013 plenary meetings promised to give the market "a decisive role." Current premier Li Keqiang, far from claiming the economy has solid prospects, has repeatedly said needed reform will be as painful as cutting one's own flesh.[23]

This is certainly better than the burst in public investment that inaugurated the Hu Jintao government. And a reforming, thriving China can still be achieved. But strong words are hardly enough. Neither the reforms implemented to date nor those promised will reverse stagnation. In fact, the reform re-start praised by many was fundamentally flawed from the outset.[24]

Greater labor mobility could mitigate aging's blow to growth by letting the right workers move freely to the right jobs. China still discourages labor mobility by denying education, pension and other benefits to those living and working in the 'incorrect' place. Pledged changes to this system retain many barriers between rural and urban areas until 2020 and keep the most popular urban centers cordoned off to those born elsewhere.[25] This may be due to continued fear of labor migration breeding social instability. If so, the Party will restrict labor markets indefinitely despite China aging.

---

[21] Regina M. Abrami, William C. Kirby, and F. Warren McFarlan, "Why China Can't Innovate," *Harvard Business Review*, March 2014, https://hbr.org/2014/03/why-china-cant-innovate.

[22] Kristijian Lucic, "ZTE Decided To Sue Huawei Due to The Alleged Camera Tech Infringement," Android Headlines, April 22, 2015, http://www.androidheadlines.com/2015/04/zte-decided-sue-huawei-due-alleged-camera-tech-infringement.html; Derek M. Scissors, "Making the new normal meaningful," *China Policy Review*, March 2015, https://www.aei.org/wp-content/uploads/2015/02/Making-the-new-normal-meaningful.pdf

[23] Jason Subler and Kevin Yao, "China vows 'decisive' role for markets, results by 2020," *Reuters*, November 12, 2013, http://www.reuters.com/article/2013/11/12/us-china-reform-idUSBRE9AA0YB20131112; Emma Rowley, "China's new premier Li Keqiang 'to cut state control over economy'," *The Telegraph*, March 17, 2013. http://www.telegraph.co.uk/finance/china-business/9936059/Chinas-new-premier-Li-Keqiang-to-cut-state-control-over-economy.html

[24] Derek Scissors. *China's economic reform plan will probably fail*, (Washington: AEI. 2014). https://www.aei.org/wp-content/uploads/2014/02/-chinas-economic-reform_130747310260.pdf

[25] Jingxi Mo, "China introduces guidelines for household registration reform," The State Council of the People's Republic of China, July 30, 2014. http://english.gov.cn/news/news_release/2014/08/23/content_281474983030658.htm; Richard Silk, "China's hukous reform plan starts to take shape," *The Wall Street Journal*, August 4, 2014, http://blogs.wsj.com/chinarealtime/2014/08/04/chinas-hukou-reform-plan-starts-to-take-shape/ .

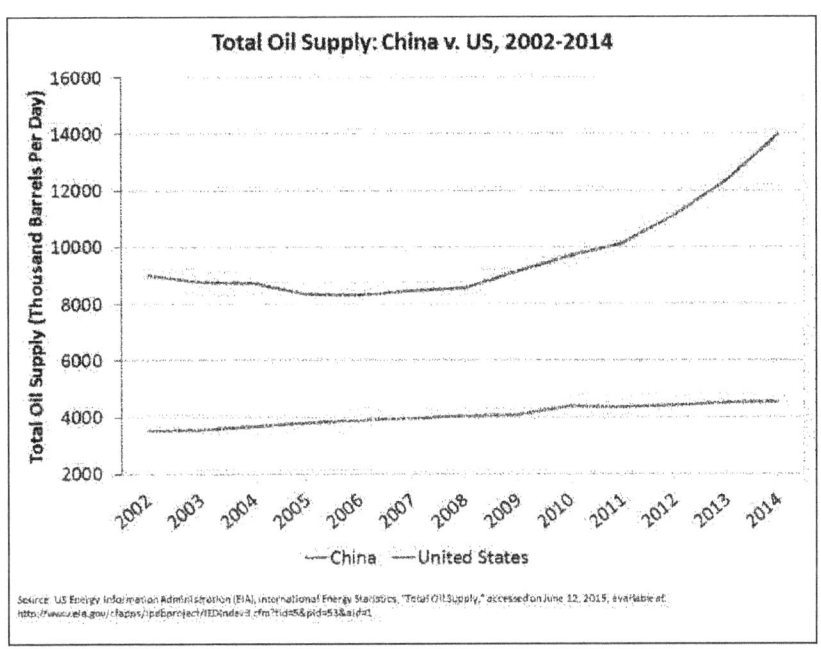

Reform could sharply increase the value of China's natural resources, along the same lines as in the U.S. China has the shale to vitalize its energy industry and curb import dependence. But this would require mimicking the American model at least in part, involving private ownership of rural land, an end to the state's energy monopoly, and legal protection of innovators.[26] The reform platform and actions to date show no progress in any of these areas. It is true that outright environmental damage is being reduced but this translates to less harm to future growth, rather than a boost.

There has been some market reform in finance. The most important element is the issuing of bank licenses to private companies. While interest rate liberalization wins headlines, it has little value when so much of the financial system still must follow the Party's orders.[27] What is needed is the truly commercial, not political, lending that can only come from independent institutions. The licenses could bolster the return on capital, and thus growth.

---

[26] U.S. Energy Information Administration. *Technically recoverable shale oil and shale gas resources: An assessment of 137 shale formations in 41 countries outside the United States*, (Washington DC: US EIA, 2013), http://www.eia.gov/analysis/studies/worldshalegas/ and Dan Blumenthal *et al, Too much energy? Asia at 2030*, (Washington, DC: AEI, 2015), https://www.aei.org/publication/much-energy-asia-2030/

[27] "China readies for private banks," *China Daily*, March 11, 2014, http://www.chinadaily.com.cn/china/2014npcandcppcc/2014-03/11/content_17340179.htm; "China tells banks to step up lending to lift flagging growth," CNBC, December 11, 2014, http://www.cnbc.com/id/102262475.

Nonetheless, by themselves they are completely inadequate. It could take decades for private banks to substantially erode the state's 90 percent share of banking assets; all the while, unsound lending will be creating a colossal amount of debt. Much more radical action is necessary. One possibility is allowing money to leave the country freely, which would pressure financial institutions to be more responsible or lose assets.[28] For this to greatly improve financial efficiency, however, liberalization must be total. Fearing rapid and heavy capital outflow, the Party has to now always opted for only partial liberalization.

The state sector is the clearest area of reform failure. The Party's pledges here go in precisely the wrong direction. Rather than shrinking the state sector to make room for private competition, they call for private investment in SOEs and state-led projects. This is essentially an attempt at a private bailout of the public sector's mistakes. Further, rather than being allowed to fail or be sold off, SOEs are being merged with each other to get even bigger.[29] There is no sign of the market being given a decisive role in the corporate sector, quite the opposite.

This error affects innovation. Beijing sees super-large SOEs as offering advantages in competition overseas.[30] But faced with no competition at home, these firms have no reason to innovate. Chinese consumers will therefore continue to be discouraged by inferior products and prices and the state giants will progressively lose ground overseas, no matter their size. Only private Chinese firms, forced to compete both at home and overseas, will succeed fully. If reform does not include a smaller state sector, innovation will be stunted.

20 State-led Industries

Autos	Armaments
Aviation	Banking
Coal	Construction
Environmental technology	Insurance
Machinery	Media
Natural gas	Non-ferrous metals
Oil	Petrochemicals
Power	Railways
Shipping	Steel
Telecom	Tobacco

---

[28] "China to push on with capital account opening: central bank deputy chief," *Reuters*, November 3, 2014. http://www.reuters.com/article/2014/11/03/us-china-economy-capital-account-idUSKBN0IN09R20141103
[29] "China encourages private capital," *Xinhua*, November 15, 2013. http://news.xinhuanet.com/english/china/2013-11/15/c_132891965.htm; "China's Huafu Group swallowed by COFCO Corp.," *Xinhua*, November 26, 2013, http://news.xinhuanet.com/english/china/2014-11/26/c_133816435.htm.
[30] Michael Lelyveld, "China mulls major industry mergers," Radio Free Asia, April 11. 2015, http://www.rfa.org/english/commentaries/energy_watch/mergers-05112015101557.html.

Brief Implications

China began to wander off the market path in 2003 and has not yet returned. Unless it does, growth will halt by the end of this decade, regardless of what the government claims. This has many economic and political implications. While stagnation is far from certain, it is likely enough that the U.S. should be preparing.

An indispensable, if perhaps boring, step is to avoid making the same mistake made with the Soviet Union, whose decline was missed until very late. The U.S. needs a concerted effort to compile statistics on the Chinese economy that are as independent as possible of those published under the Party's auspices. This will help explain Chinese behavior that will otherwise seem mysterious or, worse, surprising.

A stalled China will be more a lost opportunity than a dangerous development for the U.S. economically. American financial exposure is comparatively minor. China's trade role as a gigantic but low-margin manufacturer is a luxury, rather than a necessity; other countries played this role before and can again. The enormous opportunities many hoped for as China grew wealthy will not materialize but the country will still be very large and have nearly bottomless needs for elderly care and environmental technology, among other things. American companies will see fortunes shift, but government action is unnecessary.

An interesting twist is that stagnation could induce heavier Chinese investment in the U.S than if the country was thriving. Lack of opportunities at home could push Chinese firms and individuals to seek greener pastures elsewhere, forcing American policy-makers to decide how much Chinese investment is wanted and in what fields.[31]

Some American friends and allies will suffer more from Chinese economic weakness; indeed, energy and metals exporters around the world already have. The obvious policy response is for the U.S. to try to build its trade and investment ties with countries such as Australia and Brazil, as well as large parts of sub-Saharan Africa.

In strategic terms, a stagnant China does not guarantee American global leadership. Instead, it guarantees that either the U.S. provides global leadership or there is none. The dollar provides the most prominent example. A China that does not fully liberalize capital movement is more likely to stall. The RMB will then fall well short of challenging the dollar and the dollar's future as the world's reserve currency will remain almost entirely in American hands. This implication applies broadly.

---

[31] Derek Scissors, *China's outward investment healthy, puzzling* (Washington, DC: AEI, 2015), https://www.aei.org/publication/chinas-outward-investment-healthy-puzzling/

Mr. SALMON. Thank you.

Mr. Han.

STATEMENT OF MR. HAN DONGFANG, FOUNDER AND DIRECTOR, CHINA LABOUR BULLETIN

Mr. HAN. Thank you, Mr. Chair. Likewise, I enjoyed our conversation in Hong Kong. I am here as a democracy activist based in Hong Kong for more than 20 years and fighting for better labor rights protection and democracy in China.

I want to share with you what is behind the South China Sea conflict. What is changing, what is possible in China's society. Ten years ago, the China Labour Bulletin decided to go for a collective bargaining system in workplaces, and we fight for that instead of political freedom of association to take what the Chinese Government doesn't want to give.

So during the 10 years, the first 5 years we did seminars and writing articles to promote this idea, but in the last 5 years we got involved into 70 strike cases, we are able to make each of the 70 cases into a certain level of collective bargaining. And that proves something, that when we made that decision people were doubting, without freedom of association, whether you can do collective bargaining under a communist regime. We did so.

So 10 years after, I have to say very proudly collective bargaining in workplaces in China is being accepted by different people in this country, including the government and official trade union and labor NGOs, and most importantly, the workers who are on strike. From wildcat strike without a clear agenda, without a clear strategy, they turn into very a clear strategy on their collective bargaining. So that makes labor relations much less confrontational than before.

So that means if collective bargaining can happen under a communist regime, and the labor issue and labor movement even can be operated at some level in China, that was the most sensitive issue in the communist regime, if that can happen, I think there are many other things that can happen. If the government can allow these things to happen, many other things can happen. So I just want to share with you about that, and there are possibilities.

And the second point I want to share is that China is a highly interest-oriented country. So you have a military, you have a Public Security Bureau, you have the state security, and you have workers, you have employers. And this country is highly operated with a market economy. So how can we deal with a highly self-interested society and politics as well? And that is one of the reasons, I have to say, why the labor movement became possible under the communist regime.

And the other point I want to make is social media with the new technology. This is no longer as a tool. Social media is no longer as a tool. It is a way of living for hundreds of millions of Chinese people. That means controlling information for anyone, including the government and security, it is not possible. And hundreds of millions of Chinese people are receiving and sending out information, sharing information, sharing their desperation, their experiences with others over the Internet either with people they know or they don't know.

So the new reality, the social media, really, really provided a huge opportunity and space for civil society to grow, and that is what I believe the future democracy and China's change will be based on. So therefore I would like to recommend to people who are working on the China-U.S. relationship, I would like to see as a democracy activist, I would like to see the U.S.-China relation have less hostility and more trust, and I really would like to see to build a strategic partnership, even in the South China Sea. Why not? It is possible.

And second, I would like to see the U.S. devote more resources to help China develop the civil society movement, which is already growing, for example, the labor movement development. It will benefit both the U.S. workers and Chinese workers to have both sides higher income.

So therefore I want to emphasize that the CCP, Chinese Government, is already changing into a new reality, and I believe China doesn't need to repeat what happened in Eastern Europe countries and the former Soviet Union. It can change the country for the better. So I would like to say that the civil society movement, it is very vulnerable and fragile, if anything happens between the U.S. and China military-wise, and that will be a disaster for the civil society to develop.

Thank you, Mr. Chair.

[The prepared statement of Mr. Han follows:]

HAN Dongfang
Executive Director, China Labour Bulletin
Committee on Foreign Affairs, Subcommittee on Asia and the Pacific
June 17, 2015, China's Rise: The Strategic Impact of Its Economic and Military Growth

The sight of China's President Xi Jinping seated next to Russian President Vladimir Putin at the military parade in Moscow two month ago to commemorate the 70th anniversary of the end of World War Two in Europe must make many people in the West uncomfortable. A strategic, alliance between Russia and China would not be in the interests of the United States and its allies.

I do not believe China intends to create such an alliance. President Xi's presence at the Moscow parade has more to do with promoting his image as a military leader and his political standing inside China than with threatening other states. The same is true of his tough stance on Japan and the islands in the South China Sea; President Xi has to bend with the increasingly nationalistic wind in his own country and demonstrate that he is willing and able to defend China's territorial integrity.

THE INSECURITY OF THE CURRENT REGIME

The reason President Xi is so focused on building his support at home is simple: his position is not yet secure. Many overseas observers see President Xi as a Putin-like man, determined to get his way on everything, eradicate dissent and exert maximum control over the political, economic and social landscape. This view says more about our own fears than it does about the reality in China. The reality is that President Xi is a man who may not yet in full control and whose political position is under constant threat due to the unprecedented anti-corruption campaign he has undertaken.

The current insecurity of the Chinese administration has sources other than the anti-corruption campaign. For one, they can no longer control China's economy despite their more sophisticated grasp of macro-economic tools. The economy is now dominated by the market and the interests of private capital and property, and the Chinese Communist Party (CCP) leadership has to listen to those interests rather than command them, as was the case in the days of the state-planned economy.

Society has also changed and become more pluralistic and vocal as more people speak out and even demonstrate on the street about environmental degradation, wages and working conditions, sexual harassment, discrimination, corruption and other socioeconomic problems. These issues are disseminated and discussed among millions of Chinese thanks to the rapid growth of new technologies, the internet and social media. These developments mean that the communist regime is much less able to suppress society compared to ten or even five years ago.

Indeed, China now faces its greatest domestic challenge since 1949. Its policies lack a strong ideological justification. It is still ruled by the biggest remaining Communist regime on earth but its economic, social and political policies have little to do with communism or socialism. In addition, even as China's economic power grows, the worsening corruption in daily economic activities such as the privatization of state-owned enterprises in major industrial cities and massive illegal land grabs in the countryside, and the fast growing gap between the rich and the poor, have dramatically reduced the regime's legitimacy.

President Xi was going in the right direction with his very important 3rd Plenum Decision in 2013. That Decision promised to carry out much needed economic, financial and social reforms. For the first time, a major policy document spoke about creating a system of social governance based on rule of law that would involve working together with other stakeholders in society, such as NGOs, to address China's governance challenges.

However, right now, we see precisely the opposite happening. China is in the middle of a massive crackdown on civil society activists and organizations. Lawyers, scholars, journalists, NGO leaders, and women's rights advocates have all been detained, beaten or harassed simply because they chose to exercise their rights to free speech and assembly. In addition, laws are being drafted on counterterrorism, national security and foreign NGO management, all of which will strengthen the powers of the security and police forces.

In terms of winning popular support, these developments make no sense at all. It is not in the CCP's interests to crack down on civil society. I can only conclude, going back to what I said about the insecurity of President Xi's position, that these actions are merely further evidence that he is not fully in charge of the country's security force and faces significant constraints on his power.

One of those constraints comes from powerful, competing interest groups in China, both within the official power structure and in society. One of the most powerful interest groups in China is the police and security forces. The country's security apparatus sees civil society groups as a threat. In their eyes, giving civil society a more prominent role and voice will undermine their power within the political structure. So when China's political leaders sought to encourage the growth of civil society by better regulating it through the idea of "social governance," the Public Security Ministry and others took that opportunity to smash civil society. It is damaging to the civil society of course. This is also a dangerous situation for President Xi, because in any authoritarian society, before the political leadership has not yet in full control, the security forces will always place their own interests above those of whoever happens to be in power at the time.

Another vested interest group is the official union – the All-China Federation of Trade Union (ACFTU). When President Xi told the ACFTU leadership in late 2013 that they should do more to improve the lives of workers so that they can achieve their "China Dream", the ACFTU listened politely and, rather than carry out any substantive reforms, responded by making its usual statements about cultivating model workers. This will benefit neither the interests of Chinese workers nor President Xi, but only the entrenched interests of more than one million full-time ACFTU officials.

In order to survive in this environment, the CCP leadership needs to rediscover the source of its ideological legitimacy and it needs allies, in particular support from Chinese citizens. President Xi's campaign against corrupt officials is a great way to win popular support but there is no way it can succeed unless the CCP is willing to include ordinary citizens and civil society organizations in that campaign, and allow them to take part in supervising official wrongdoing.

BUILDING A NEW SOCIAL CONTRACT BETWEEN THE CCP AND WORKERS

While the police and the ACFTU are reluctant to help Xi Jinping realize his China Dream, there is one very important socioeconomic group that is emerging as a natural ally of the CCP - China's workers. It is the workers and farmers, many of whom have migrated to China's cities to become the main part of the country's growing working class, who were the CCP's core constituency during its revolutionary period. It is the workers who are now pushing for social change and justice and a better standard of living for China's working class. Everyday in China, workers are going on strike demanding better pay and working conditions, and the pension and medical insurance they are supposed to receive but are denied by their employer. And every day they go on strike to demand these fundamental rights, they are met by the police who block their way and by trade union officials who are more concerned with sweeping the dispute under the carpet than in helping workers address their demands.

This is the first time in the history of modern China that the interests of the CCP and the workers have been fully and beneficially aligned. In the past, Chairman Mao Zedong, who was operating from a position of strength, was able to use the workers as a political tool to further his own goals but now the situation is different. It is the CCP that needs the workers on board to achieve the common goals. In the process, the CCP has an historic opportunity to return to its original socialist vision and revitalize its ideological credentials.

I see this opportunity for a new social contract between the CCP and China's workers because of the transformation that we witness in southern China where most of our labor organizing work takes place. This transformation came about because of a strategic decision that we made at China Labour Bulletin ten years ago to change the direction of our work. I would like to tell that story here.

Ten years ago was a very different time for labor in China when it was still regarded as one of the most sensitive issues in the country. At the same time, wildcat strikes were growing in number. The main reason for these strikes was that unfairness and labor rights violations in the workplaces had reached an unsustainable level. Many workers were unable to support their families and willing to take the risk to make their voice heard. Local governments did not know how to respond other than to use police and security forces to crack down on striking workers. In most cases, organizers were arrested and sentenced to prison. Employers quickly realized that they did not need to respond to the workers' demands because the government would continue to arrest the organizers for the sake of maintaining political and social stability and in line with the longstanding policy to deny workers the right to organize.

We began to see a vicious circle emerge: workers continued to go on strike in order to support their families, local governments continued to arrest strike organizers because this was the only thing they knew how to do, and employers did not need to make any effort to avoid strikes because they knew that the government would send in the police. As a result, there were not many choices left for workers but to continue to go on strike.

At first, this new reality made our work much more exciting and heightened our sense of importance because there were more cases of worker injustices to expose to the international community. We could continue to condemn the Chinese government for suppressing workers and denying them the right to organize and strike. We could also try to submit these cases to the International Labour Organization (ILO) to put pressure on the Chinese government.

But then several other developments began to intrude on this reality and made us start doubting whether our conventional way of working was really effective in changing the behavior of the Chinese government, and improving life for workers and prospects for the labor movement.

First, the Cold War had come to an end and with it, the global struggle between the West and East. Second, globalization became the dominant global reality and relations between states focused increasingly on trade and economic issues. Third, the majority of the hundreds of millions of workers in China either did not know about the ACFTU, or did not believe that it represented them simply because it had never been helpful to workers in the past.

Robin Munro, a good friend and colleague of mine, used to tell me to jump out of the box when you feel you are trapped. When you look back at the box that you jumped out of, you will then be able to see what was inside the box that was keeping you from coming up with good ideas.

So I jumped out of the box at that point and started to ask myself questions.

Did Chinese workers make any political demands in their strikes? The answer was no. In fact, in all their strike actions, workers were only asking for legally entitled overtime pay and benefits. They wanted to raise their salary to a level that reflected their labor and ensure their family's livelihood.

If most workers did not feel their demands were politically sensitive, then why would everyone else believe so? By everyone else, I include government officials, labor scholars, political scientists and journalists, Chinese labor NGO leaders, my fellow dissident friends, and of course, me and my colleagues at China Labour Bulletin. I believe that this sense of political sensitivity was heavily affected by the impact of the Solidarity movement in Poland in the 1980s, which was the beginning of the end of the Communist regimes in Eastern Europe. Ironically, Chinese workers never seemed to think that their action could be related to the Solidarity movement in Poland. If then, in the eyes of the Chinese workers, the mission of the labor movement in China was not to end the Communist regime, what should it be?

After raising these questions, we decided to be brave and make a strategic decision to change the direction of our work: instead of trying to put an end to the Chinese Communist regime, the next stage in China's labor movement should focus on introducing collective bargaining into workplaces.

Our thinking was that the future development of China's new labor movement needed more time to go through the same developmental process as the trade union movement in Europe and North America during the late 19th and early 20th century. Of course, the labor movement in China did not need another 100 years to develop and mature, but we did need a long enough period of time to lay a solid foundation to ensure that the trade union would be able to carry out its heavy responsibilities: to ensure that China's hundreds of millions of workers and their families could improve their lives, and that a country with the world's largest population and over a thousand years of violent revolutionary history would be able to evolve peacefully into a prosperous, stable social democracy.

At a political level, we believed that the issue of workers' rights, trade union rights and workplace democracy in China should be detached from the issue of CCP rule, and focused instead on the issue of all social classes are able to share resources in a fair and just way. In other words, by targeting workplace collective bargaining, rather than freedom of association, we would change the discourse on the labor issue, separating it from regime change, and connecting it to social justice.

In this way, we would be able to depoliticize an overly politicized labor issue, transforming it into what it was originally: a socioeconomic issue. We decided, on our way toward the future, instead of seeing the Communist regime as an enemy, we would see them as a potential partner who was still fearful and therefore hostile towards the labor movement, a partner who needed time to build up the confidence to let go of its unnecessary fears. We decided that we also needed time to build up enough confidence to deal with this hostile partner. We believe that over time we could reduce this level of hostility and forge a partnership with the CCP that would benefit the Chinese people and nation.

In 2005, when China Labour Bulletin decided to switch our focus to introducing workplace collective bargaining in China, most of my friends laughed and wished me good luck. No one believed that workers could claim the right to collective bargaining without first getting the right to freedom of association, especially under a Communist regime.

My visits abroad have convinced me that our decision was the right one. I am lucky to have traveled to many countries around the world over the past 20 years, meeting with labor activists and trade unionists. Every time I visit a trade union abroad, especially one in a democratic country, people keep telling me how difficult it is for unions when it comes to collective bargaining. I began asking myself: will that be the case if one day we have freedom of association and democracy in China? If so, then why not start by making collective bargaining a reality, and worry later about the union?

There were other concerns and criticisms about our change in strategy. Among the international trade union movement, people were worried that our decision to back off on freedom of association might damage the International Labor Organization's (ILO) 1948 Freedom of Association and Protection of the Right to Organize Convention (C87) and the 1949 Right to Organize and Collective Bargaining Convention, (C98). In other words, if the rights to collective bargaining could be established in China, the Chinese government could refuse to ratify both conventions and deny workers the rights to organize free and independent trade unions which has always been recognized as a fundamental right. Some international trade union friends even expressed their concerns that our strategy could make it more difficult for them to defend ILO core standards, particularly those on the rights to freedom of association.

Beside the international trade union movement, my fellow dissidents friends had their own concerns. They worried that our change in strategy might prolong CCP's rule and thus the suffering of Chinese people under an authoritarian regime.

I tried to explain to my friends that workplace collective bargaining was about introducing democracy into workplaces. If a workplace collective bargaining system could be introduced in China, it would mean that workers in a wide range of enterprises could democratically elect bargaining representatives to negotiate with employers regarding wage and benefits and working conditions. That meant, even under an authoritarian regime, workers would be able to practice democracy in ways that mattered to their lives. Over time, institutionalizing this practice would put in place conditions that would push the CCP to adopt other democratizing reforms that would advance social dialogue and governance, reduce social tensions, and create a more stable and prosperous nation.

None of my friends were convinced by my argument and they politely reminded me about all the evil things that the CPC has done to our people and the nation. Who, they asked, will be held accountable for the crimes that the CCP has conducted and how will they be held accountable? How can you make sure that the CCP will finally accept a more democratic regime? How can you guarantee that eventually we will be able to abolish CCP rule in our country as people did in Eastern European countries and Russia?

I have not been able to give satisfactory answers to many of these questions raised by my international trade union and Chinese dissident friends. I apologized to them and went ahead with the plan to change our strategy to push for workplace collective bargaining in China.

I told my friends from the international trade union movement to see Geneva and China as two fronts in the battle. They would hold firm in Geneva and we would make the breakthrough in China. I explained to my fellow dissident friends that Chinese workers should not have to wait for the fall of Communism to see improvements in their working conditions and in their families' lives. Our change in strategy would ensure that the beautiful promises of the CCP would be realized step by step, even though it might very possibly prolong Communist Party rule.

While I have not been able to adequately answer the questions of my friends and critics, what I can say to them is that China Labour Bulletin has achieved much of what we set out to do ten years ago. We have developed a strong network of labor NGOs inside China who are highly committed to promoting workplace collective bargaining system. In the last five years, we have now been involved in more than 70 collective bargaining cases and successfully redirected confrontational strikes through a collective bargaining process that allows for dialogue between labor and employers. We have helped thousands of workers elect their representatives democratically during strikes and set up a system that allows workers to hold these representatives accountable. We have conducted trainings in China and Hong Kong that bring worker representatives together from different factories to share both their success stories and failures. We have organized conferences to bring together worker representatives, labor scholars, labor NGOs, lawyers, media journalists and government officials to discuss how to craft new legislation so that workplace collective bargaining can be institutionalized. We have persuaded the mainstream media in China to report on our cases in order to raise public awareness and generate public discussion of workplace collective bargaining. We have utilized China's fast-growing social media to promote solidarity and organizing among workers. We have produced documentary films on workers who have contracted devastating occupational illnesses such as pneumoconiosis in workplaces but have not been able to get their legally entitled compensation in order to push for legislation improvement. We are now in the process of producing another documentary film profiling worker leaders who have been engaged in labor organizing and collective bargaining work.

I am proud to say that our work over the last ten years has made a number of contributions to China's present and future development. It has helped reduce the fear among government officials and ACFTU officials of workplace collective bargaining. It has helped them to understand that China's well-developed labor laws can be better implemented if more organized workers are willing to standing up to fight for justice. Collective bargaining is now recognized by a growing number of officials, scholars, NGOs and workers as an effective way to solve labor disputes, avoid unnecessary strikes, reduce hostilities between workers and employers and contribute to China's social and political stability. Our work has also helped us to persuade other labor NGOs focused on social service provision, charity and CSR to re-orient themselves as

NGOs dedicated to labor organizing and advancing the labor movement in China. Finally, it has helped empower many workers from factories, the public service sector, retail stores and construction sites who no longer see themselves as passive victims of injustice but as fighters and agents of change to rectify those injustices.

All of this progress has been made possible because of the decision we made ten years ago to depoliticize the labor issue and turn it into a socioeconomic issue linked to collective bargaining. It was also made possible by our willingness to see the CCP as a party willing and able to learn and continue the reform process, and as a potential partner with whom we could find common ground to work together to better the lives of the Chinese working people and Chinese nation.

THE CASE FOR U.S.-CHINA ENGAGEMENT: ADVANCING THE LABOR MOVEMENT AND THE FUTURE OF SOCIAL DEMOCRACY IN CHINA

Given the progress that we have seen taking place on the ground, I believe that there is now a golden opportunity for China's workers and the CCP to work together and create a fairer, more equal and stable society, just as the workers, trade unionists and social democratic parties of northern Europe did in the late 19th century and early 20th century. It is absolutely essential that the CCP seize this opportunity, not just for its own sake but for the sake of China and the international community. What happens in a country as large as China, with a population approaching one and half billion that consumes energy and resources from all over the world, is clearly going to impact the global economy. China's hundreds of millions of workers have already demonstrated this point by lowering the value of global labor during the first three decades of China's economic reform. We hope our work on collective bargaining will reverse that trend and contribute to raising the value of global labor over the next three decades while, in the process, creating peaceful mechanisms to advance social dialogue and governance. It is important to remember that China is a country with a long and violent revolutionary history, and it is in everyone's interests to make sure that history does not repeat itself. A stable, more just and secure China is critical for global peace, security and sustainability. Our work on collective bargaining will make a small contribution to this goal, but to go further we need the help of the U.S. and the international community to ensure that China will enjoy a peaceful external environment for carrying out domestic reforms that will be beneficial to China's workers and civil society.

Broadly speaking, there are now three paths that China could follow: Become like Russia, a dictatorship in which might is right, basic rights are discarded and ordinary citizens are left out in the cold; become a consumerist, free-market economy that sucks up the world's resources and destroys the global environment; or become a social democracy that provides for its own citizens, maintains balanced and sustainable economic growth and protects the environment.

It may be tempting to want to see China take the second route, but that would be courting economic and ecological disaster. Clearly, it is everyone's interests, including the United States, to support and encourage China along the third path.

The United States should not see China as threat. Do not let that photo-op with Putin in Red Square distract you. Now is the time to engage with China, to build trust and develop a long-term and mutually beneficial relationship with China. A key element of that process will be continued support for, and collaboration with, civil society. The current crackdown will fade but the long-term need to foster a fair and just society will always remain.

Mr. SALMON. Thank you.
Mr. Cohen.

STATEMENT OF MR. JEROME A. COHEN, PROFESSOR AND CO–DIRECTOR, U.S.–ASIA LAW INSTITUTE, NEW YORK UNIVERSITY SCHOOL OF LAW

Mr. COHEN. I want to congratulate the chairman and members of the committee for opening statements that were eloquent, comprehensive, and stimulating, and I think I have learned a lot just from listening to my two colleagues.

My own remarks will focus first on the domestic scene, and secondly on China's foreign policy, which is our most immediate problem.

On the domestic scene, I think between the chairman's statement and what we have heard here, I don't have to recite a whole chain of challenges, but it helps to remember them because I am neither on the side of the collapsists who think China is on the verge of demise or those who think China is going to dominate the world. I think actually, because its vulnerabilities are accumulating and beginning to outweigh its assets, that China may have peaked in terms of the world's fear of China and respect for it.

It doesn't mean, however, that this government is going to disappear. When we remember the example of North Korea, even they are able to hang on indefinitely. So we shouldn't underestimate the viability of this government, but we have to think about what it is likely to do.

The sad thing from the point of view of China's leaders is these people represent a Communist Party that after 65 years of ups and downs really has to be credited with making huge economic and social progress. On the other hand, the speed of that progress has led to many of their problems. They are victims of their own success, and they have not devised a system that is adequate for dealing with these questions, whether you call it democratic or democratic dictatorship or whatever. And these leaders are afraid. They are like cats on a hot tin roof. Despite their many accomplishments, they fear overthrow. And June 4, 1989, in which Mr. Han took part, was a too vivid reminder for them.

So they engage in repression, and the repression has gotten worse in the last 3 years under Mr. Xi Jinping. He will appear here in September, a very attractive character, able person. But the fact is we have to understand the repressive policies in which he is engaged. I have many friends in prison in China. I have many who are exiles who cannot go back to China. These are often the cream of Chinese society. They are the best future of China.

Repression cannot go on forever. If we look at the example of Taiwan, when I first went to Taiwan in 1961, Chiang Kai-shek's son was head of the secret police. He was a killer. By the mid-1980s, when he was in charge of the government he had inherited from his father, he was beginning to be a modernizer. He saw you can't go on using repression. You have to begin to develop social, economic, political, and legal institutions that can process the grievances that accumulate inevitably with progress. And he started off what now has become the vibrant democracy in Taiwan.

And that is something I wish Mr. Xi Jinping and his colleagues could expend more energy on. But their natural turn is repression. And we are going to see this perhaps for 8 more years if he can remain in office, despite his anticorruption campaign's implications, et cetera. I think somebody has to assert the time has come for domestic reform of a serious nature.

But let me talk about the international situation. You know, it is easy to exaggerate, with the current concern over China's policy toward the South China Sea, how terrible their foreign policy may be, et cetera, but we really need to keep an overview. And I think China and the U.S. are ready to continue cooperation on many subjects, particularly environment, climate problems, et cetera. I think with the coming Strategic and Economic Dialogue we will see continuing efforts to compromise on many of the controversial issues that plague us.

China has entered the WTO in largely a constructive way, and although it hasn't completed complying with all its obligations, I think that is a good example of China as a full participant in the world process. On the other hand, as was mentioned, the so-called foreign NGO law that is being prepared is going to wreak havoc with China's foreign relations. It is going to cover much more than NGOs. Every university is covered. Their definition of NGO is very, very broad.

And the institution in China that is going to administer this is the Ministry of Public Security, the police, not the Ministry of Civil Affairs that used to be responsible for these problems exclusively. And that may be the best hope for seeing revisions of the law before it is passed, because other Chinese institutions are very jealous of the authority of the police organizations in China. And we should note, the budget for the police organizations in China exceeds, every year now, the budget for the national military. That is a pretty sobering reflection of the repression that is going on.

But the most important questions are serious ones that plague us today. It used to be the East China Sea with Japan, but it is noteworthy we don't hear much about that now, and there is a lesson in that, because we could see the same result if we play our cards right with the South China Sea.

It seems to me the South China Sea issue has to lead to what to me as a international law professor and lawyer is very obvious. Different countries have different views about the rights and wrongs of the international law issues involved about the specs of Earth and the Spratlys and Paracels, et cetera. The obvious answer, as it is in the East China Sea between Japan and China, is turn to international law. Turn not only to assertions that we are right and there is no dispute we are right because we are right, that is just nonsense. International law also presents institutions for resolving these questions.

We don't have that when we look at cyber attacks, we have no rules yet for that, and we have no institutions for applying those rules. But we do have that with the Law of the Sea. That is what UNCLOS is. And I hope that you will try to use your influence with the Senate to make a final successful effort for the U.S. finally to accede to UNCLOS, because right now we are denied the opportunity to do what the Philippines has done.

I admire enormously what the Philippines has done. They had the guts to bring China to an arbitration under the Law of the Sea institutions, and China is legally committed to take part and certainly to observe whatever decision comes out of these impartial experts who are arbitrating the Philippine dispute with China.

Early next year we will at least have a decision whether this tribunal has jurisdiction over the case, and I think it will probably find it does have and it will go on to answer some of the questions that currently plague us. Do you want to know what an island is compared to a reef, compared to a rock? These questions may well be answered through the Philippine arbitration. Is the nine-dash line a bunch of hooey, as many of us think it is? Well, we can look to the Philippine arbitration perhaps to answer that. This is just an example of what international law institutions can do if they are invoked.

The sad thing is the Philippines stands by itself right now. Japan may be saying: We will hold your coat and we hope you win. That is certainly Vietnam's view. And we have others. Taiwan, of course, is excluded from formal participation, but they too should be taking initiative. This is the time for using international institutions and imagination.

There are so many ways available, in the light of international law precedents, for solving these problems. You can decide to do an inventory of all these features and decide which are reefs, which are rocks, which are islands entitled to a full panoply of Law of the Sea benefits, Continental Shelf, exclusive economic zone, and all that. We can have diplomats decide we will divide up, we will share jurisdiction, we will share resources in some ways.

But the diplomats are in a stalemate. We have heard the use of stalemate to describe the domestic situation in China, stalling. Well, we have a stalled political situation internationally, and the United States and Japan and Taiwan, as well as the Philippines, and even Vietnam, which behind the scenes sides with the Philippines, have to use the existing institutions, and I hope that your committee will use its influence to make more of the opportunities that exist.

So that is the burden of what I have to say.

[The prepared statement of Mr. Cohen follows:]

Jerome A. Cohen

Professor and co-director of the US-Asia Law Institute at New York University School of Law

Adjunct senior fellow for Asia at the Council on Foreign Relations

China's Future - and Our Own

Statement Before the House Committee on Foreign Affairs, Subcommittee on Asia and the Pacific:

"China's Rise: The Strategic Impact of Its Economic and Military Growth"

June 17, 2015

Mr. Chairman, I am grateful for the opportunity to address the momentous question of "The Future of China", especially since, increasingly, China's future and our own are inextricably linked. In these brief opening remarks, I will discuss China's internal situation, then its external relations.

THE INTERNAL SITUATION

Forecasts of China's future run the gamut. I do not endorse either extreme. There is no significant chance that in the foreseeable future the Communist government will follow the fate of the Soviet Union. Nor do I share the view that the People's Republic is becoming so powerful that it will dominate the world.

Despite its remarkable recent achievements, China's economic, social and political problems are many and growing. It is possible that Beijing's performance may now have peaked. Its accumulating problems and failure to develop a political system adequate to deal with them may soon be seen, both inside and outside the country, to constrict its further progress and the deployment of its impressive assets.

Many a Chinese leader must think it a cruel twist of fate that a regime that has done so much to improve the living standards of hundreds of millions of people should be so obviously frightened about its continuing viability. Yet the Communist Party can be seen as a victim of its own successes as well as its apparent failures. No country can modernize as rapidly as China without suffering the enormous consequences of immense social change.

Rather than basking in the gratitude of a contented nation, Xi Jinping and his colleagues have revealed themselves to all the world as cats on a hot tin roof. Their pomp and propaganda at home and abroad cannot conceal their fear of overthrow or disintegration. Their attempt to limit the impact of Western values, ideas, institutions and practices, embodied in the current draft legislation to restrict foreign cooperation in education, civic affairs and politics, is a deeply embarrassing and shameful public confession of the fragility of their system.

Having benefitted from several decades of the "open policy" initiated by Deng Xiaoping, his fear-mongering successors now want to cut off the "ideological infiltration" they believe threatens their "democratic dictatorship". If successful, this new policy will inhibit China's ability to respond to domestic and global demands. As my colleague Ira Belkin recently noted, "It's a bad 1960s policy for a 2015 challenge".

Because of the system's non-transparency, Xi Jinping knows far better than we do the vulnerabilities underlying China's formidable achievements. Staggering pollution, massive corruption, labor unrest, unfair land transfers, growing income inequality, arbitrary bureaucracy, ethnic tensions and invidious social discriminations, increasing persecution of human rights lawyers and civil society reformers, a Party-dominated judiciary, and ever greater curbs on social gatherings, journalism, the Internet and social media are fuelling discontent and resentment that a now significantly troubled economy and an anticipated stock market crash can ignite. As Chairman Mao admonished, and the June 4, 1989 Tiananmen tragedy demonstrated, "a single spark can start a prairie fire".

Yet repression offers no long-run solution and cannot last forever. In the mid-1980s, Taiwan's Chiang Ching-kuo, although heir to his father Chiang Kai-shek's Leninist party dictatorship, recognized that secure progress requires gradual political reform and launched the process that transformed Taiwan into a vibrant democracy. China needs similar enlightened leadership today.

Understandably, China's Communist elite is far from united in how to confront its many challenges. Despite General Secretary Xi's attempt to impose monolithic controls on the Party, the first three years of his rule have exposed major cracks in the leadership. The life prison sentence meted out behind closed doors last week to China's formerly feared national security chief, Zhou Yongkang, is only the most recent evidence of a continuing power struggle as well as the operation of the Party's "socialist rule of law with Chinese characteristics". The Chinese people, who have generally supported Xi's persisting campaign to reduce official corruption, are waiting to see whether he is willing to risk further elite dissension by pursuing corrupt leaders who, unlike Zhou, have not been his political rivals. At the same time, many Chinese are hoping that Xi will moderate his repressive course and gradually lead them toward reforms that will give full play to their prodigious capacities.

FOREIGN POLICY

Although China's increasingly "assertive" international conduct has naturally stirred widespread concern in both Asia and this country, especially regarding the South China Sea, an overview of Beijing's foreign policy suggests a less alarming perspective. In some major subjects, such as environmental pollution and climate change, there are good prospects for Beijing's cooperation with the United States and other nations. Next week's annual Sino-American Security & Economic Dialogue should illustrate the continuing ability of the world's two economic super-powers to develop compromises regarding trade, financial and investment problems that inevitably arise. Despite certain compliance issues, China's participation in the WTO has, on the whole, been positive, as has much of its direct investment in an expanding list of countries. Indeed, through its newly-established Asian Infrastructure Investment Bank and related organizations , Beijing is now pursuing an innovative and constructive financial course, to the embarrassment of our own government.

Beijing as well as Taipei should also be given credit for the past seven years of cooperation across the Taiwan Strait that have significantly improved stability and security in Asia. But the impending departure from office of Taiwan's President Ma Ying-jeou and growing Taiwanese fears of the Mainland dictatorship's threat to the island's democracy should alert us to the forthcoming renewal of earlier tensions.

Of course, we do not see eye-to-eye with China on a number of controversial issues including North Korea, the Middle East and Ukraine, and evolving Sino-Russian relations generally require our greater attention. Yet other issues raise even more serious challenges.

Among the most abiding is Beijing's continuing violation of obligations it has assumed in over twenty international human rights treaties and related documents. The proposed legislation designed to restrict the activities of foreign NGOs and educational organizations mentioned above will surely have a further adverse effect on Beijing's international relations. Coming to grips with the devastating cyber attacks now being attributed to China - and the much less-publicized American cyber attacks on China - may prove to be the most difficult topic confronting our two governments, since, as yet, there are no specific international laws or institutions for dealing with it.

Most immediately threatening to our relationship, however, is today's drama in the South China Sea. Here, fortunately, the United Nations Convention on the Law of the Sea (UNCLOS) does provide not only rules for determining conflicting maritime claims but also legal institutions for impartially applying those rules. In 2013, the Philippines, in a desperate attempt to invoke law as a defense against overwhelming power, stunned China by bringing an UNCLOS arbitration challenging Beijing's expansive and vague "nine-dash line" and seeking to confirm crucial distinctions between submerged "reefs", bare "rocks" and credible "islands". The arbitrators' decision promises to clarify the legitimacy and legal consequences of the troublesome Chinese "land reclamation" projects that have profound military implications.

Thus far, unfortunately, China, while seeking to defend its actions in the realms of propaganda and scholarship, has refused to submit to the independent arbitration tribunal's jurisdiction. These impartial experts are expected to rule on their jurisdiction this winter. If China thumbs its nose at an adverse decision and a subsequent determination of the merits of the dispute, it will be in blatant violation of UNCLOS obligations that it freely ratified after taking an active part in the long negotiations preceding the treaty.

As recently underscored by Singapore's distinguished legal expert Tommy Koh, who presided over the successful conclusion of the UNCLOS negotiations, China, in flatly rejecting all opportunities for peaceful settlement of maritime as well as territorial disputes through international arbitration, adjudication and other third-party procedures, is plainly out of step with the practices of other Asian countries and the rest of the world. To be sure, impartial dispute resolution often cannot replace negotiations, but it can always do much to narrow the issues and stimulate as well as inform diplomats who have thus far failed to propose and agree upon the imaginative solutions that are urgently required.

The present crisis in the South China Sea has a significance that goes far beyond the immediate claims involved. If China -. and the United States, which has not yet even acceded to UNCLOS - cannot agree upon and respect in practice mutually beneficial rules and institutions for peacefully settling disputes, the future of both countries and the world community will surely be gloomy. This issue must be placed high on the agenda for Xi Jinping's visit to Washington in September!

A CONCLUDING THOUGHT ABOUT CONTEMPORARY CHINA

For centuries, foreign observers of "the Central Realm" have emphasized their own concerns. Not surprisingly, I believe that one of the themes connecting Beijing's domestic and foreign policies today is insufficient recognition of the importance of a pluralistic society and the legal institutions required to promote it. "Rule of law" is a term of many meanings that has often been abused. But China would benefit at home and abroad by demonstrating increasing respect for its core meaning – government under law. And the United States, by striving harder to set a good example, could do much to improve not only our own society but also our standing in China and the world.

This message is intended only for the use of the Addressee and may contain information that is privileged and confidential. If you are not the intended recipient, you are hereby notified that any dissemination of this communication is strictly prohibited. If you have received this communication in error, please erase all copies of the message and its attachments and notify us immediately.

Mr. SALMON. Thank you very much.

Dr. Hersh.

STATEMENT OF ADAM HERSH, PH.D., SENIOR ECONOMIST, ROOSEVELT INSTITUTE

Mr. HERSH. Thank you, Chairman Salmon, Ranking Member Sherman, thank you for inviting me to testify today.

China's rising geoeconomic and geopolitical significance and what it means for the United States could not be a more timely or important topic, particularly as our Nation considers how to proceed with the Trans-Pacific Partnership trade agreement.

Let me begin with a point of agreement on this issue. The rules for how our economy works, who gets to write those rules, this is of fundamental importance to the United States' economic future. The divisions we saw in last week's historic TPA/TAA vote here in the House reveal how much the rules matter to people. Some point to this outcome as a sign of a broken Congress, but I submit this was Congress doing its work.

Rather, what is broken is the relationship between Congress and the executive branch, particularly the USTR, and how divided constitutional authorities to make international agreements work in practice in our Government. When the rules matter this much, we should take the time to get them right, rather than trying to bulldoze through Congress whatever rules USTR and the corporate lobbyists that negotiate these agreements with them, supposedly on our behalf.

What we know about this agreement is that it has less to do with freeing trade, creating jobs, raising wages, or rebalancing geopolitics than it does with rewriting the global economic rules to favor corporations, CEOs, and shareholders at the expense of almost everybody else. Unless Congress acts to change this balance of power with the executive, we should expect more of the same confrontational politics and uncertainty over policy when what we really need is to reach agreements that meet our national imperatives through cooperation and inclusion.

I will make two points today. My first point is that the most fundamental thing for national security is a strong national economy, and TPP would weaken our economic base, leave us more unequal overall, and reinforce the global race to the bottom in social and environmental standards, commercial standards, and taxation. My second point is that TPP fails the geostrategic rationale for checking China's rise on many fronts.

On my first point, estimates of TPP's economic impact say it would raise U.S. GDP by $88 billion by the year 2025. This amount is less than the statistical rounding error when we calculate GDP for the United States. If each of you chose a pet infrastructure project in your district and decided to fund that, it would have a bigger economic impact over the next year than TPP will have 10 years from now.

TPP's big changes are not to lower traditional barriers between countries, but to change how the economic rules work within countries. I detail this in more detail in my written testimony, but I will highlight the investor-state dispute settlement as one of the major issues of the agreement.

Here I will note that progressives like Senator Elizabeth Warren and my boss, Nobel Prize-winning economist Joseph Stiglitz, are aligned with scholars from the Cato Institute and editors from The Economist magazine in agreeing that ISDS goes too far in empowering global corporations against the sovereignty of the public to regulate in its interest. What ISDS does is provide an implicit subsidy for foreign investors to move their investments offshore and makes it more difficult for our partners to raise the standards that we say we care much about.

My second major point is that TPP fails the geostrategic rationale for keeping China in check. This is a 20th century cold war containment strategy aimed at a 21st century problem where the United States is no longer the center of the world economy. For this to work, it would need to do two things. It would need to truly set high standards and it would need to largely exclude China from the benefits of this trade bloc. This would let TPP countries get a bigger share of the supposedly higher standard trade and investment happening in the region and entice China to raise itself toward TPP standards, but it does neither of these.

On the first test, TPP makes no meaningful advances over the status quo of recent trade agreements. It leaves in place the same woefully toothless mechanism to enforce standards on labor rights, environmental protections, and accountability for state-owned enterprises. And TPP foregoes the opportunity to discipline currency manipulation for trade advantage, which is a pervasive practice, not just in China but across the Asia region.

On the second test, TPP cannot feasibly exclude China from the benefits of the agreement. China is already more integrated with TPP countries than the United States. Its total trade with non-NAFTA TPP members is nearly double that what the United States has with the same group of countries. What this means is that either by investing directly in or trading Chinese-produced content through TPP countries, deeper and growing integration with China will mean that Chinese producers can enjoy access to TPP's market access without reciprocating the same market opening to U.S. businesses and workers. In fact, the Chinese officials I talk to are about as enthusiastic for TPP as any business lobbyist here in Washington.

China's transformation under authoritarian capitalism, its ongoing nonmarket economic structure, its expanding geopolitical influence, these all pose real challenges for the United States and for the future of open societies around the world. But TPP does not provide answers to these challenges.

Finally, our own unforced errors in foreign economic relations are much for damaging the U.S. reputation in the region than your vote on TPA and slowing down the process for negotiating TPP. Here, I am looking at things like Congress' failure to enact internationally negotiated IMF reforms and to this administration's diplomatic debacle in trying to strong-arm our allies into boycotting China's Asian Infrastructure Investment Bank. When this is how we treat our friends, it is no wonder the United States has a reputation problem in the world.

This strategic choice cost us an opportunity to write the economic rules with China. Instead, it left us isolated from the international community and left China to write the rules on its own.

These problems do not end with TPP. A multitude of other agreements are underway with the same basic template, from a mega regional agreement with the European Union, to the trade in services agreement, to bilateral investment treaties with China itself. These will determine whether we grow with broadly shared prosperity or continue down our economic path that produces high and rising inequality and low economic opportunity.

Strengthening international relations is essential for ongoing U.S. leadership in the world. So is getting these rules right. No American should relish a failure to build deeper and more open relations with our partners, nor should we retreat from trying. But getting to a deal that serves more than the narrow interests of powerful multinational corporations requires that Americans be willing to walk away from the TPP agreement that we have on the table now.

Thank you.

[The prepared statement of Mr. Hersh follows:]

*Testimony before the United States House Committee on Foreign Affairs,
Subcommittee on Asia and the Pacific, Hearing on China's Rise: The Strategic Impact
of Its Economic and Military Growth*

June 17, 2015

Dr. Adam S. Hersh, Ph.D.
Senior Economist, Roosevelt Institute and Visiting Scholar at Columbia University's
Initiative for Policy Dialogue

Chairman Salmon, Ranking Member Sherman, members, thank you for inviting me
to testify on this pivotal topic: the geo-economic and geo-political significance of
China's rapid development and the U.S. strategic response, particularly as it pertains
to the Trans-Pacific Partnership agreement.

I would like to begin on points of agreement between proponents: it matters a lot
who gets to write the rules for how our economy and the international economy
work. Last week's historic vote by you and your colleagues on Trade Promotion
Authority and Trade Adjustment Assistance showed how much the rules matter.
What this said is that something is broken in the ways the United States makes trade
rules: the dysfunction of the implicit agreement between Congress and the
President—and his delegated ambassador as United States Trade Representative—
in how Constitutional division of authorities to make international agreements will
govern in practice.

When the rules matter this much, we should take the time to get them right, rather
than bull-doze non-transparent new rules through Congress. What we know about
the agreement—from Wikileaks, and from conversations with negotiators of more
open TPP countries—is that the Trans-Pacific Partnership (TPP) has less to do with
freeing trade, creating jobs, raising wages, or rebalancing geo-politics than it does
with rewriting the rules of global trade and investment to favor big businesses at the
expense of almost everyone else in society.[1]

These rules do not embody economic principles of open competition so much as the
preferences of industry lobbyists that had the best seats at the U.S. Trade
Representative's table. The outcome is an agreement that fails to address America's
economic needs and geostrategic goals. Legitimate concerns have been raised on the
left, right, and center of the American political debate, only to be dismissed by
conventional wisdom as protectionist, old-fashioned, or naive to the ways of the
world. But as Larry Summers wrote in the *Washington Post*, it's time to take these
concerns seriously.[2]

Problems with current U.S. model for trade policy do not end with TPP. A multitude of agreements are underway under the same basic template--from a parallel mega-regional agreement with the European Union, to a multilateral agreement on trade in services (TISA), to a bilateral investment treaty with China itself and other countries that will all be critical to the U.S. economic future. They are critical to whether we grow with broadly shared prosperity or continue down the path of an economy producing high and rising inequality, and low economic opportunity.

Proponents of TPP are asking us to believe we can achieve the high road outcomes from a USTR so captured by special interests. But unless Congress acts to change the rules on how the United States government negotiates international economic agreements, we can expect the same confrontational and uncertain political outcomes, rather than a cooperative, inclusive approach to setting national economic priorities.

I will make two points today:

1. The most fundamental element of national security is a strong national economy, and TPP would weaken our economic base, leave us more unequal, and reinforce the global race to the bottom in social, environmental, and commercial standards and taxation.

2. TPP fails the geostrategic rationale for checking China's rise.

On the first point, the most generous models predicting TPP's economic impact claim it would raise U.S. GDP by $88 billion (in today's prices) by 2025.[3] This amount is less than the rounding error when the Department of Commerce calculates GDP. If you each picked an infrastructure project in your district, together you would create a bigger growth impact in the next year than TPP would have ten years from now.

The United States ranks among the highest of the advanced economy countries in inequality, and among the lowest in terms of upward economic mobility. TPP will lead to higher inequality--adjustment to new terms of trade will focus job and small business elimination in more labor-intensive industries—not just manufacturing, but in services of increasingly higher skill—faster than trade creates them in less labor-intensive export-expanding industries. Recent research by MIT economists Daron Acemoglu, David Autor, and co-authors shows that such import shocks decimate local economies, causing higher unemployment, slower wage growth, and straining social expenditures and tax revenues. Trade with China in particular, they estimate, cost the U.S. economy 2 to 2.4 million jobs over the course of the 2000s.[4]

TPP goes far beyond mere tariffs and trade. All sides agree TPP's most significant provisions address "behind the border" measures—not what happens between countries, but how the economic rules will work within countries.

To highlight two major issues, first is TPP's investor–state dispute settlement mechanism (ISDS). Here, progressives like Senator Elizabeth Warren and a Nobel prize-winning economist Joseph Stiglitz are joined by the likes of Cato Institute and *The Economist* magazine in raising concerns that ISDS serves to empower global businesses against public regulation.[5] Understandably, global businesses would like assurance against expropriation and discriminatory treatment where rule of law is underdeveloped. But they can already buy private insurance against such risks. That USTR also insists on ISDS in an agreement with Europe, where no one questions legal standards, reveals the lie that this is about protecting investor rights, rather than expanding and subsidizing them.

The distortions created by this change in the rules provide a privilege for foreign investors not accessible to domestic investors in any TPP market, and works against developing country partners growing their own institutions and organically raising standards through more open, democratic policymaking. The combined result is to further incentive production to move offshore.

We also have to be clear about the dangers of TPP's expansive intellectual property protections. Economic research is clear that patents do not increase innovation or growth. Rather, they serve to raise consumer prices and restrain competition. The agreement reportedly will allow "ever-greening" of drug patents and aim for more stringent exclusivity for biosimilar medicines than even President Obama's budget proposed, meaning less access to medicines and slower development of new ones in TPP members and in third party countries. For the United States, this outcome would mean more national income will be spent on health care—through private spending and public programs. This is not a question of guns versus butter, but of guns, butter, or life-changing medicines.

On my second major point, that TPP fails the geostrategic rationale for checking China's rise, proponents argue TPP is needed to buttress Asia-Pacific allies with an implicit economic ring-fence around China's rising power and influence. This is a Cold War containment strategy, but in the 21st century the United States is no longer the epicenter of the world economy. And the strategy violates a seemingly forgotten long-standing tenet of the open world trading system, built painstakingly under U.S. leadership in the postwar years: the quest for peaceful foreign relations would be built on the principle of not excluding countries from the benefit of economic relations—the opposite of what TPP, and the Trans-Atlantic Trade and Investment Partnership would do.

A strategic agreement countering China's rising influence, to be effective, requires two things: First, it must truly set high standards for international trade and investment; second, it must largely exclude China from the benefits, diverting investment and trade to TPP countries, thereby enticing China to rise to TPP standards. TPP does neither. China's economic transformation under authoritarian capitalism, it's ongoing non-market economic structure, and its expanding geopolitical influence pose real foreign and economic challenges for the United States and for the future of open societies, but TPP doesn't answer to any of them.

On the first question, the level of standards, TPP clearly does not make any economically meaningful advances over the status quo. Although the agreement reportedly would establish well-sounding obligations on labor rights, environmental protection, and accountability for state-owned enterprises, TPP provides no credible mechanism to enforce these standards.

The lose-lose scenarios created by non-credible enforcement mechanisms are best illustrated in the case of Guatemala. In April 2008, Guatemalan workers first filed complaint of systemic labor abuses with the U.S. Department of Labor, as established by the US-Central American Free Trade Agreement; it took the USTR until December 2014 to open a formal dispute settlement case, and a ruling is still far off. Other recent experiences with partner countries Honduras and Colombia show no better results of improved practices or even an end to the rampant murders of free trade union members. This is the worst of both worlds: U.S. workers and businesses still face race-to-the-bottom competition, while global businesses and developing country governments face little pressure to improve conditions. No one has yet to give a clear answer to how TPP will effect free labor standards in one-party state Vietnam, or deter human trafficking of labor in Malaysia or Mexico?

This toothless model of enforcement for things other than investment and commercial disputes—and the fact that the agreement will not discipline currency manipulation in the Asia-Pacific region show that TPP does not set standards at a level that would pose meaningful constraints on China's economic behavior.

On the second question, TPP cannot feasibly exclude China from the benefits of the TPP bloc. In fact, Chinese officials and technocrats are as enthusiastic about TPP as any business lobbyist in Washington. That's because the 1 percent in both countries stand to gain substantially from a deal allowing both to expand supply chains into lower-cost developing Asia. TPP will not lock-in a U.S. export advantage in the region so much as a platform for U.S. and Chinese companies that want to offshore production to TPP member countries. This loophole is found in TPP's "Rules of Origin," or the percentage of a product's value must be created in the TPP member country in order to qualify for preferential access to U.S. markets.

China is already more integrated with TPP countries than the United States. China's total trade (exports plus imports) with non-Nafta TPP partners is nearly double ours--$780 billion in 2014 for China to our $423 billion.[6] Beijing is now incentivizing Chinese enterprises in a strategy of "going out"—expanding China's global footprint and brand recognition through massive foreign direct investment.

Deep and growing integration with TPP countries will mean that Chinese producers can enjoy the agreement's benefits—either by investing in or trading Chinese-produced content through TPP countries, without reciprocating to TPP's preferential terms. How big an economy is and its geographical proximity to others—the "gravitational factors"—matter much more for international trade patterns than do agreements like TPP. China's economy will be bigger, grow faster, and be geographically and culturally closer to Asia-Pacific countries no matter what we do.

What's more, TPP offers negligible counterbalance to the soft power China is earning in the region with its efforts to develop new models of multilateral infrastructure development financing. Here, America's own unforced errors in foreign economic relations—from Congress's failure to enact internationally negotiated IMF reforms, to this administration's diplomatic debacle in their miscalculated strategy of strong-arming allies into a global boycott of China's efforts to advance multilateral development finance institutions with the Asian Infrastructure Investment Bank and other projects. This U.S. strategic choice actually lost us an opportunity to write the economic rules with China, instead the strategy left us isolated from the international community and left China to write the rules of these multilateral institutions without us.

When this is how we treat our friends, it's no wonder the United States has a reputation problem in the region. To illustrate the challenge, consider that Chinese officials and scholars routinely raise the Opium War and 1842 Treaty of Nanjing in conversations on trade and investment relations; they named their regional trade development initiative the "New Silk Road Initiative"—this is an area of the world where reputation holds long historical memory. Between the new BRICs bank, the Asian Infrastructure Investment Bank, and China's Silk Road investment initiatives, China is committing $300 billion of capital investment, and buying untold foreign influence. TPP simply does not match the same return on investment on the political capital we have spent pressing our partners to ignore the same concerns that make trade such a contentious political issue in the United States.

There is a further lesson here: America's economic future is tied more to the choices we make in the rules of our own economy rather than joining agreements. This Congress has been reluctant to invest in our own infrastructure. China's leaders not only recognize the growth value from investing in their own economy, but in helping other countries develop in ways that create mutually-reinforcing trade and growth benefits for China. This is what it means to treat countries like true partners rather than geopolitical pawns.

Conclusion

Strengthening international relationships is essential for ongoing U.S. leadership in the world—be it economic, political, or cultural. No American should relish a failure to build deeper, more open relations with foreign partners, nor should we retreat from trying. But getting to a deal that serves more than the narrow interests of powerful corporations, their CEOs and shareholders will require Americans be willing to walk away from the agreement we have now, and for Congress to change how it exercises input and oversight over USTR's negotiating priorities.

---

[1] Full disclosure: I have been briefed privately, off the record on a number of occasions by USTR officials, but am similarly prevented from revealing the substance of those discussions.

[2] Larry Summers, "Rescuing the free-trade deals," *Washington Post*, June 14, 2015, available at http://www.washingtonpost.com/opinions/rescuing-the-free-trade-deals/2015/06/14/f10d82c2-1119-11e5-9726-49d6fa26a8c6_story.html.

[3] Author's analysis of http://www.iie.com/publications/pb/pb12-16.pdf.

[4] Daron Acemoglu, David Autor, David Dorn, Gordon H. Hanson, Brendan Price , 2014, "Import Competition and the Great U.S. Employment Sag of the 2000s," *NBER Working Paper No. 20395*, available at http://www.nber.org/papers/w20395.

[5] See *Economist*, "The Arbitration Game," October 11, 2104, available at http://www.economist.com/news/finance-and-economics/21623756-governments-are-souring-treaties-protect-foreign-investors-arbitration; Simon Lester, "Does Investor State Dispute Settlement Need Reform?" *Cato Unbound: A Journal of Debate*, May 11, 2015, available at http://www.cato-unbound.org/2015/05/11/simon-lester/does-investor-state-dispute-settlement-need-reform; Joseph Stiglitz, "Where progressives and conservatives agree on trade: Current investor-state dispute settlement model is bad for the United States," Letter sent to Congressional leaders, May 18, 2015, available at http://www.rooseveltinstitute.org/joseph-stiglitz-and-trans-pacific-partnership-tpp.

[6] Analysis of United Nations Comtrade Database data, available at http://comtrade.un.org/data/.

Mr. SALMON. Thank you.

Dr. Kaufman.

STATEMENT OF ALISON KAUFMAN, PH.D., SENIOR RESEARCH SCIENTIST, CHINA STUDIES DIVISION, CNA CORPORATION

Ms. KAUFMAN. Thank you very much for having me here today. I am going to give the usual caveat that the views I express are my own, not those necessarily of CNA, the United States Navy, the Department of Defense, or in fact anyone but myself. So I state that for the record.

In my testimony today I have been asked to talk about Chinese security affairs, and the first point I want to make is that actually, in the Chinese view, everything we are talking about today is part of security affairs. Xi Jinping has been very clear about that, but it is actually quite a longstanding trend in Chinese views, that internal security, external security, economics, diplomacy, law, military, all of it is part of what they consider to be their security problem.

And so when Chinese decisionmakers think about securing their nation, they are also thinking about how to balance all of those things with one another. So I would assume that when Chinese decisionmakers sit down they actually say: Here are all these problems we have, how are we going to make these work together to strengthen China and make it more powerful?

That said, I have been asked today to talk more on the military side of things and more traditional view of security. So today I am going to raise three questions. First, what are some of the security issues that Chinese leaders appear to be worrying about the most right now? Second, what are they doing about them? And third, what does this mean for the United States?

So first, what are Chinese leaders worried about? They draw their worries from the past, the present, and the future. All countries do this. The Chinese are especially concerned with the past in many ways for shaping their view of what the future may hold. Based on the past, they worry that China's sovereignty, its territory, its international stature and reputation, its self-determination, and its internal stability are always, constantly, under threat. It is a very deep existential anxiety. There is also a longstanding view that Western powers, in particular the United States, have vested interests in China maintaining a degree of insecurity. So this is a starting point, I think, for many aspects of U.S.-China relations.

Based on the present, they look around them, and they worry that China's global interests are now expanding faster than their own ability to secure those interests. China's economic growth, especially, increasingly depends on the ability to protect overseas investments and workers—we heard a little bit about that today—to secure sea lanes that carry its energy and trade, and to manage transnational crisis and national disaster.

Then, looking to the future—and here we are lucky that China's Government and affiliated organizations have very recently published fairly authoritative texts outlining what sorts of problems they think the future holds, not just for them but for the world—they see a world in which crisis that could escalate to conflict or war lurks everywhere, in which security issues are very, very complex and transnational and will often require cooperation and coordination, both within the Chinese establishment and also with foreign countries, and in which their ability to win at information-based warfare is going to require advanced capabilities in the maritime, cyber, and space domains.

So what are they doing about these security concerns in the military domain? Obviously, you are very familiar, I think, with the military modernization program that has been going on for many years. The annual DOD report to Congress, I think, summarizes that very, very well.

In addition to that, the Chinese People's Liberation Army, the PLA, has a very, very long task list. Again, they published it recently. I would not want to have that long a task list. Of course they are supposed to be very good at warfighting and, of course, solidify any reunification with Taiwan. They are also supposed to take on crisis management, international security corporation, internal security, humanitarian assistance, disaster relief, rights and interest protection, which is both a new and an old language, support for national economic development, and a whole host of other things.

This is a very long list that they have to undertake, and Xi Jinping clearly does not think the PLA is ready to take this on. So in addition to the longstanding military modernization program, Xi also has announced dozens of areas of institutional reform within the Chinese military. Among others, it is a very long list, but among others this includes improving joint operations doctrine and capabilities, rebalancing the force structure more toward maritime, air force, and second artillery—their strategic nuclear force—building up defense R&D, improving their human capital, which has been a longstanding concern, and also improving the PLA's internal discipline and reaffirming its party loyalty.

These are all tasks that Xi has set before them in 2013, and in the intervening couple of years, and I think going forward for the next several, we are going to see a lot of changes coming out of the institutional aspects of the Chinese military.

We have also, obviously, seen the reorganization of China's civilian maritime law enforcement organizations—we have been hearing a lot about that—their white hulls, using nonmilitary vessels to conduct law enforcement operations, and also the establishment of a top-level national security commission or committee with Xi Jinping at the head whose exact mandate is still rather unclear to us.

China has also been undertaking these moves to secure what it calls its maritime rights and interests, particularly in the South China Sea. I am not going to belabor that because I think everyone is very familiar with those points. But one point to make there is that those moves, of course, make neighboring countries very unhappy. And partly in response, they are also investing now in their white hull capabilities, their civilian coast guards, things like that, and in some cases their military capabilities, and they are also enhancing their military partnerships across the region and beyond, including with the U.S.

So what does this mean for the United States? Well, I think a key challenge for the U.S., for the United States Government, for policymakers is figuring out how to manage these insecurities within the U.S.-China relationship. That doesn't necessarily mean conceding to or accommodating these insecurities, but it means encouraging China's productive cooperation and a greater sense of security in areas where those concerns are convergent with U.S. interests, and dissuading China from feeling more secure in areas where these concerns and interests may diverge from those of the United States.

Obviously, in areas such as counterpiracy, peacekeeping, non-combatant evacuations, avoiding accidental crises, all of these problems that go along with China's expanding global economic footprint, there are a lot of areas in which it may make sense to support a more secure China. A China that is more invested in burden sharing on things like counterpiracy, peacekeeping, and so on, may be more aware of the cost of losing those opportunities. A China that feels included in international efforts, including international legal institutions, as some of the other people here have been talking about, may be less suspicious of international partners, more willing to speak with them within those venues, and also less likely to strike out on its own.

That said, obviously, the way that China is currently going about dealing with many of its other security concerns is not compatible with U.S. policy and interests, and China's leadership has framed a lot of those issues in terms that would make it very hard now for them to easily walk back. This language of rights and interests is very powerful in China. It is hard for them to step back from it now that they have employed it.

Here, I think the U.S. path needs to be to show China that, in fact, China's own security interests, all the interests we talked about here at the table, are actually at cross-purposes, that China can't secure some of those interests through its current approach without seriously compromising some of the others. So China can't simultaneously maintain stable economic relations with its neighbors or with other countries in the world while aggressively pursuing its territorial claims.

China can't expect international law to work for it sometimes and not accept its jurisdiction at other times. And China can't expect other countries to simply accept that PLA modernization is not a threat without engaging in much greater and more credible transparency about the PLA's capabilities and intentions.

The costs of these self-contradicting behaviors should be high, and they should be a focal point, in my opinion, for U.S. discussions with China and U.S. cooperation with other countries in the region. I believe that the U.S. should be prepared to use all instruments of national power in tandem, economic, diplomatic, military, other instruments, to persuade China of what these costs might be.

Thank you.

[The prepared statement of Ms. Kaufman follows:]

Prepared Testimony by

Alison A. Kaufman
Senior Research Scientist, China Studies Division, CNA

To the House Committee on Foreign Affairs
Subcommittee on Asia and the Pacific

Hearing entitled
"China's Rise: The Strategic Impact of Its Economic and Military Growth"

June 17, 2015

"At present, the national security issues facing China encompass far more subjects, extend over a greater range and cover a longer time scale than at any time in the country's history."

—Chinese President Xi Jinping, 2014[1]

Chairman Salmon, Ranking Member Sherman, and Members of the Subcommittee: Thank you for this opportunity to share my thoughts with you on "China's Rise" as pertains to Chinese security affairs. I want to note that the views I express in this testimony are my own and do not reflect the views of CNA, any of its sponsors or affiliates, the United States Navy, or the Department of Defense.

I have been asked to discuss Chinese security issues. I would like to focus on issues that are especially pertinent to understanding and interpreting the *future* of China as a security actor, in the Asia-Pacific region and in the world.

There are four main points that I wish to make:

- First, for China's leadership, "national security" encompasses *many* domains, not just military and defense, and it includes both internal and external security.

- Second, to understand the Chinese leadership's outlook on security issues, we need to understand how these issues have been defined, shaped and framed by China's historical experiences, and how China's security interests are evolving today.

- Third, China's leadership is currently taking action in multiple domains to become more capable of securing these interests. This includes initiating major, far-reaching military reforms. However, PRC leaders still have significant concerns about their country's ability to safeguard its security interests.

- Finally, a major issue for the United States going forward is whether and how the U.S.-China relationship can manage China's insecurities in a manner that is convergent with U.S. interests.

I. The PRC leadership's definition of national security

The first thing I want to draw your attention to is how China's leadership defines "national security." In the Chinese view, "national security" is extremely broad. In fact, it encompasses *all* the areas that are being discussed at this hearing today—internal stability, economic growth, political legitimacy, and the more traditional area of national external defense.

Chinese views of national security today are consistent with long-standing norms there that interlink (a) China's domestic and international security, and (b) the security of the Chinese Communist Party (CCP) with the security of the Chinese state and people. Xi, as with all of the

---

[1] Xi Jinping, "A Holistic View of National Security," Speech at the first meeting of the CPC Central Committee's National Security Commission, 15 April 2014, in Xi Jinping, *The Governance of China* (Beijing: Foreign Languages Press, 2014). p. 221.

PRC's leaders, does not view the security of the nation as distinct from the security of the CCP. Because the Party is viewed as the vanguard and indisputable leader of the Chinese people, military, and state, none of the other domains can be secure if the Party's leadership is not secure. Therefore, China's primary security issue going forward will continue to be the CCP's ability to maintain its monopoly on political power.

The breadth of PRC conceptions of "national security" is usefully illustrated by a speech that Chinese President and CCP Secretary General Xi Jinping gave in his 2014 address to the new national security committee whose establishment he announced in late 2013. Xi said in that speech that "we must maintain a holistic view of national security" such that

> "We must pay close attention to both traditional and non-traditional security, and build a national security system that integrates such elements as political, homeland, military, economic, cultural, social, science and technology, information, ecological, resource, and nuclear security."[2]

There are two critical implications that come out of this conception of national security. First, we should always expect to see China's leaders prioritizing domestic security—that is, the indisputable leadership and stability of the Chinese Communist Party over the country's people, territory, government and military. External security is important to the Chinese leadership in part *because* it allows the CCP to maintain its internal legitimacy.

Second, the "holistic" view of national security means that we should expect the Chinese leadership to use every instrument of national power to secure what they perceive to be China's security interests, assuming they have the institutional and material capacity to do so.

II. China's past, present, and future security concerns

There are three key sources for how China's leaders frame their security concerns: (1) China's *past* as a divided, subjugated nation; (2) security interests that have emerged over the past few decades or are *presently* emerging as a result of China's expanded global footprint; and (3) China's changing assessments of the *future* nature of warfare and the conflicts China is most likely to face. I will discuss each of these in turn.

Since the mid-19th century, China has been deeply insecure about its ability to safeguard its national rights, interests, and dignity

To understand China's future as a security actor, we first need to look backwards. Modern China's identity as a nation-state is premised on a *deep existential anxiety* about the government's ability to sustain internal stability and external sovereignty. The PRC's and CCP's modern identity are built around a narrative of loss and redemption in which modern China was forged out of a crucible of shame and suffering at the hands of foreign powers.[3] This is

---

[2] Xi Jinping, "A Holistic View of National Security," pp. 221-222.

[3] I have written in more detail on this topic elsewhere. See Alison Adcock Kaufman, "The 'Century of Humiliation,' Then and Now: Chinese Perceptions of the International Order," *Pacific Focus* XXV: 1 (April 2010), 1–33, doi: 10.1111/j.1976-5118.2010.01039.x; and Alison A. Kaufman, "The 'Century of Humiliation' and China's National

part of the PRC's founding narrative, in the same way that colonial Americans' chafing under British taxation and their subsequent battle for independence is part of ours. *I want to emphasize that understanding these beliefs does not mean condoning them*, but it does help to highlight the issues that may be most sensitive for Chinese policy-makers today.

Some key points are:

- This narrative interprets the period between the mid-1800s and the mid-1900s as a "Century of Humiliation" during which China failed to secure its most basic national interests. Internal rebellions threatened the legitimacy of the central government, and foreign powers forced China to open its ports to foreign trade and to relinquish large portions of its territory to foreign concessions and extraterritorial jurisdiction. China lost a humiliating war to Japan in 1895. By the 1920s, China's imperial government had collapsed, the new republican government controlled just a third of the territory that China had held a century earlier, and China's confidence and pride was deeply wounded. Chinese scholars and politicians, at the time and since, bemoaned China's inability to protect its self-determination, international status and "rights" as a sovereign nation.

- According to this narrative, it was the CCP and its armed branch, the Red Army (the precursor to the modern People's Liberation Army, or PLA), that "saved" China from foreign predations and internal chaos, restored most (but not all) of its historical territory, and put China back on the path to self-determination and international standing.

- As a result of this history, the goal of all PRC leaders has been to ensure China's "national rejuvenation," i.e. its recovery from these losses and indignities. With regard to the international arena, "national rejuvenation" would mean that China has returned to a state where the country's rights, interests, power and dignity would be restored and its self-determination guaranteed.[4]

This history matters today for several reasons.

First, in order to understand what China's leaders want to secure in the future, we need to know what they think they have lost in the past. The Chinese preoccupation with "sovereignty and territorial integrity," for example, comes directly from the historical memories—revived generation after generation—of being unable to secure China's territory against foreign intrusions and predations. With regard to Taiwan, in particular, the sense is that China's wounds from this difficult past will remain open until the two sides of the Strait are reunited under CCP rule.

Of note, the *content* of the concept of "sovereignty and territorial integrity" appears to be somewhat flexible. Until fairly recently, almost the entire focus was on Taiwan, and threats to

---

Narratives," Written testimony for the U.S.-China Economic and Security Review Commission Hearing on "China's Narratives Regarding National Security Policy," March 10, 2011, http://www.uscc.gov/sites/default/files/3.10.11Kaufman.pdf.
[4] The phrase has gotten a lot of attention under Xi Jinping, who has linked the term to his "China dream," but in fact Hu Jintao, Jiang Zemin and Deng Xiaoping all used it too.

56

China's claims over islands and features in the East and South China Seas were not generally called out as a separate security concern.[5] Now, those maritime features are regularly incorporated into the PRC leadership's definition of China's "indisputable territory." So we might say that China's definition of what constitutes its interests in this case has expanded, but the *justification* for why it is important has not. The language used to explain it is so fundamental to modern Chinese identity that it immediately resonates with people who are sensitive to any hint that China's "rights and interests" could be eroded. This raises the question, of course, of whether China's definition of its "indisputable territory" could expand further in the future.

Second, the Chinese concern with international status, and with the ability to participate in the international arena in a state of "equality and reciprocity" with great and small powers, is genuine. For many decades both prior to and after the establishment of the PRC, Chinese diplomats lobbied tirelessly for their country to have a seat at the international table. When China has gained participation or membership in major international organizations—the WTO is a good example—this has been hailed within the country not only as an important tool for improving China's material conditions, but also as a symbol of China's improved international status. This framing is potentially important for the United States, because as a central player in many international institutions, the U.S. is viewed as a "gatekeeper" for membership or enhanced participation in them. Hence U.S. encouragement or discouragement of Chinese membership in international organizations is sometimes viewed as a barometer of the U.S.'s broader willingness to allow China to regain its international dignity and standing.

Third, this history matters because these losses to China's territory, autonomy, and international standing are laid directly at the feet of foreign powers, particularly Western powers. The language that we see in many Chinese writings about international affairs today derives directly from an assumption, developed during the "Century of Humiliation," that it was in the very nature of Western great powers to seek to encroach on other countries' territories and to subjugate them in a "win-lose," zero-sum situation. There has grown from this a deep-rooted suspicion of Western intentions toward China that has been repeatedly reinforced by all PRC leaders, who say that the West seeks to deprive China of its power by stunting it in the international arena and seeking the overthrow or subversion of the Chinese communist system. Xi Jinping is no exception. What this means for the U.S. is that, no matter what we say in the short term, China's leadership is going to approach U.S. actions and relationships—particularly in the Asia Pacific—starting from a point of great suspicion.

Finally, this narrative emphasizes the centrality of military power for securing national power, autonomy, and dignity. The historical formulation is *"fuguo qiangbing"* (富国强兵)—rich nation, strong army—and Xi Jinping has recently revived this language. China's recently-issued 2015 defense white paper puts it simply: "the Chinese dream is to make the country strong. ... Without a strong military, a country can be neither safe nor strong." In other words, even if all of China's security concerns were resolved tomorrow, we would expect China to continue to strengthen and modernize its military simply as a matter of what it views as historical necessity.

---

[5] See Murray Scot Tanner and Peter W. Mackenzie, *China's Emerging National Security Interests and their Impact on the People's Liberation Army* (Arlington, VA: CNA; Quantico, VA: Marine Corps University Press, 2015), pp. 11-12, especially footnote 18.

To sum up, China today starts from a position of *deep resentment* about the loss of its rights, power, and dignity, a *deep desire* to have a central role at the international table, and *deep insecurity* about the willingness of the rest of the world to let China seek its own destiny and secure its own interests.

China's economic growth and globalization have resulted in significantly expanded national security interests

In addition to these historical anxieties, China has added a host of additional security concerns over the past several decades. First, in the 1980s, Deng Xiaoping calculated that China's major challenge in the immediate future would not be to stave off major war from outside invaders, but rather to ensure its own prosperity. This necessitated a stable, peaceful and non-hostile regional and international environment conducive to China's economic growth, and therefore gave China a strong interest in managing frictions with its neighbors and with major powers. China's leadership since Deng has sought to build peace and stability through increased participation in international institutions and economic and diplomatic outreach to neighboring countries, avoiding conflict with major powers, and expanding its military diplomacy.[6]

Even more recently, China's growing international footprint has caused its global security interests to expand. As the PRC's trade and investment with foreign nations grows and as its people go further afield as workers and tourists, China has increasingly far-flung interests that need to be protected.

Two of my colleagues at CNA identified six arenas of "emerging" national security interests that result from China's expanded regional and global presence.[7] They include the needs to:

- Protect overseas investment and Chinese working abroad
- Deepen energy and resource security
- Strengthen maritime security interests
- Stabilize China's western borderland regions
- Develop space and cyberspace security interests
- Shape China's security environment.

Each of these interests has the potential to require new missions and capabilities on the part of China's main security force, the PLA, as well as other security forces.[8] Protecting overseas investments and people, for instance, could require the PLA to conduct non-combatant evacuation operations in an unstable country. Deepening energy and resource security requires that China be able to protect SLOCs through which its energy supplies pass. Strengthening maritime security interests could require the PLA to be able to: defend China's claimed maritime territories; exploit and protect maritime resources; maintain strategic depth, access, and power projection in areas near its national coastlines; and conduct maritime security cooperation.[9]

---

[6] Tanner and Mackenzie, pp. 12-13.

[7] Tanner and Mackenzie, Chapter 2.

[8] Hu Jintao explicitly tasked the PLA with helping to manage and defend these expanded security interests in his 2004 speech on "The Historic Missions of the Armed Forces in the New Period of the New Century."

[9] Tanner and Mackenzie, pp. 47-48.

Of note, many of these expanded national interests do not necessarily conflict with those of other nations, and the Chinese recognize these as areas with potential for burden-sharing with other countries.

China's national security outlook is also shaped by the future conflicts and challenges that PRC leaders believe their country might face

Finally, China's leaders make assessments about trends in warfare and international relations, and the implications of these trends for the kinds of future challenges that China is likely to face.[10] Recent PRC strategic documents depict a world in which the possibility still exists of full-scale warfare resulting from Taiwan independence or from foreign "hegemonic countries inciting war with the goal of delaying or interrupting [China's] rise."[11] They describe a world in which conflict is increasingly likely to arise from the escalation of *crisis*, particularly as a result of boundary or jurisdictional disputes in the maritime domain. They see a world in which transnational, non-traditional issues such as terrorism, piracy, natural disasters and pandemics threaten the security and prosperity of all nations. They depict a world in which internal instability from other nations may spill over into China's territory. And finally, they portray a world in which changes in the conduct of warfare increasingly demand advanced capabilities in the maritime, space, cyber, and nuclear deterrence domains.

There are a few important implications here. First, this list suggests that China's leaders see a future where problems may be driven by crisis and by non-traditional security threats as much as by deliberate provocation. This leads to an assessment that *crisis management* is an essential strategic task in order to prevent an escalation to war.

Second, it suggests that China increasingly views distant geographical areas as directly relevant to its own security; China's military will consequently need capabilities that give it a greater reach into areas further from China's territory.

Finally, it suggests that we should expect to see China's military make a concerted effort to improve its maritime, cyber, and space capabilities. In 2012, Hu Jintao stated in his final work report as the CCP Secretary General that it was time to "build China into a maritime power."[12] The 2015 PRC defense white paper elaborated that "The traditional mentality that land outweighs sea must be abandoned, and greater importance has to be attached to managing the seas and oceans and protecting maritime rights and interests."[13] Recent PRC statements and documents have also emphasized the importance of the cyber and information domains, arguing that "information dominance" is a critical element in the management of conflict and the prosecution of war, and have noted that space is also increasingly prominent as a domain of potential conflict.

---

[10] State Council Information Office of the People's Republic of China, *China's Military Strategy* (Beijing, May 2015); Shou Xiaosong, ed., *The Science of Military Strategy* (*Zhanlue Xue*; 战略学) (Beijing: Military Science Press, 2013).
[11] *The Science of Military Strategy*, 2013, p. 99.
[12] "Full text of Hu Jintao's report at 18th Party Congress," *Xinhua*, Nov. 27, 2012, http://www.china-embassy.org/eng/zt/18th_CPC_National_Congress_Eng/t992917.htm
[13] *China's Military Strategy*, Section IV, "Building and Development of China's Armed Forces."

III. The Chinese leadership is taking steps across multiple domains to improve the country's ability to secure these interests

China's military is tasked with a very long, and growing, list of missions.

The PRC leadership's interpretation of China's history, its current expanded security interests, and its future challenges together shape the list of situations for which they feel the PLA and other national security actors must prepare. These add up to a very long list of things that the PLA needs to be able to do. The 2015 defense white paper sums them up:

"China's armed forces mainly shoulder the following strategic tasks:
- To deal with a wide range of emergencies and military threats, and effectively safeguard the sovereignty and security of China's territorial land, air and sea
- To resolutely safeguard the reunification of the motherland
- To safeguard China's security and interests and new domains
- To safeguard the security of China's overseas interests
- To maintain strategic deterrence and carry out nuclear counterattack
- To participate in regional and international security cooperation and maintain regional and world peace
- To strengthen efforts in operations against infiltration, separatism and terrorism so as to maintain China's political security and social stability; and
- To perform such tasks as emergency rescue and disaster relief, rights and interests protection, guard duties, and support for national economic and social development."

Thus the PLA is tasked not only with war preparation, but also with crisis management, military diplomacy and cooperation, internal security, and support for national economic development. A burning question for the CCP, therefore, is whether the PLA is institutionally, operationally, or politically prepared to take on this huge roster of missions.

PRC leadership is increasingly confident in China's ability to secure many of its interests, but they acknowledge that many obstacles remain

In many ways, China today is a world away from the insecure, weakened state of the Century of Humiliation. Over the past decade, official Chinese documents have increasingly declared the centrality of China as a global player. There appears to be a much greater confidence in China's international standing and power. Five years ago, there was still a raging debate in China about whether it could be, or would want to be, a "great power." Now, that debate is over and no one in China (or elsewhere) disputes that China is a major world power.

In the recently-issued 2015 defense white paper, for instance, the authors say that "China's comprehensive national strength, core competitiveness and risk-resistance capacity are notably increasing, and China enjoys growing international standing and influence."

This growing confidence is reflected in many domains. The most obvious is China's more assertive behavior in the East and especially South China Seas, where China's media and government justify activities such as building structures on marine features as essential for restoring China's stolen "rights and interests" in the maritime domain. It is possible that the PRC leadership thinks that it can now afford to take bolder steps in this area both because the PLA is more militarily capable in the past, and because China can bear greater risk to its peripheral relations and to regional stability. But we also see growing confidence in China's ability to cooperate and to burden-share, through e.g. increased Chinese participation in anti-piracy operations, humanitarian assistance and disaster relief, and sending more skilled personnel to international peacekeeping missions. And, finally, we see growing confidence in China's ability to win international support for its role as a central player in, or even creator of, international institutions, for example through the recent establishment of the Asian Infrastructure Investment Bank.

That said, the PRC leadership still thinks China has a long way to go in being able to secure all its interests, near and far. Some of these obstacles are external: they repeatedly argue, for example, that the U.S.—its dominance in international institutions, its presence and activities in Asia, and its regional alliances—presents significant challenges to Chinese self-determination.

China's leaders also recognize many *internal* obstacles to attaining their national security goals. Many of these have to do with the need to reform the PLA, as discussed in the next sub-section.

China's military and defense establishment has been ordered to take a number of steps to improve its ability to safeguard China's security

In November 2013, Xi Jinping announced wide ranging, national-level reforms at the Third Plenum of the 18th Congress of the Chinese Communist Party. These included nearly four dozen areas of reforms for the PLA. The areas covered by these reforms give us a useful snapshot of the operational and institutional areas that China's leadership have deemed most important and/or most in need of improvement. They include:

- Command and control for joint operations

- Organizational changes, including rebalancing of the force structure to put greater emphasis on the navy, air force, and second artillery; it could also entail rebalancing of the four PLA general departments, and perhaps the Military Regions

- A continuation of a long-standing concern to improve the PLA's human capital

- The desire to build "new type operational forces," i.e. key assets or units which are characterized by cutting-edge technologies and are deemed essential for prosecuting modern campaigns

- Defense R&D, acquisition of advanced weaponry and equipment, and improved "civil-military integration" that better allows civil education and technological systems to support defense priorities

- Improvement of Chinese logistics capabilities

- Improvement of the defense mobilization system, including the reserve force

- Improving the PLA's institutional management capabilities

- Adjustments to China's national military strategy

- Improvement of internal discipline and reaffirmation of Party control over military

- The establishment of a "national security commission," with Xi Jinping at the head, presumably aimed at improving the centralized management of civilian and military national security actors.

These changes are going to entail pain for many parts of the PLA. Unlike past PLA reforms, which have been announced by the Central Military Commission, these were announced at an important *Party* meeting, and Xi Jinping is at the head of the organizations apparently tasked with overseeing and pushing forward the reforms. In other words, these are not changes that are internally generated. David Finkelstein of CNA has called this the PLA's "Goldwater-Nichols moment," noting that "just as it took an act of Congress in 1986 to force the U.S. military to forge a joint organization, it would seem that the force of Xi Jinping and the Central Committee [of the CCP] are going to be leveraged to impel the PLA to do what it has long known must be done but which has proven too bureaucratically difficult without external catalyzing forces."[14]

IV. Implications for the United States

China's attempts to become more capable of securing its identified national interests present opportunities for the United States, but also many challenges. A key question to ask in assessing these opportunities and challenges is: *How can the U.S.-China relationship manage China's insecurities in a manner that is convergent with U.S. interests?*

Many of China's stated security interests are potentially convergent with those of the United States. Counter-piracy, peacekeeping, non-combatant evacuations, and issues in non-military domains such as climate change, are all broadly compatible with U.S. interests and provide opportunities for cooperation that can help to reassure China that the U.S. does not seek to block its progress in these areas. Cooperation in geographic areas outside the Asia-Pacific could be particularly fruitful, because historically China's existential anxieties do not revolve around regions outside Asia.

China's government has also been amenable to forms of cooperation that show that the United States regards China as an equal partner in the international arena. A good example is the recent signing of two U.S.-PRC memoranda of understanding, one on establishing rules of behavior for the safety of maritime and air encounters, and the other on notification of major military activities. These sorts of agreements are important not only because, if properly implemented, they can help manage the immediate danger of misinterpretation or miscommunication, but also because they show that the U.S. takes China seriously as an

---

[14] David M. Finkelstein, "2015 Should Be an Exciting Year," *Pathfinder* 13:1 (Winter 2015), p. 10.

international actor. Similarly, China's government and public have often reacted more favorably toward U.S. military activities when they include China.

However, many of the PRC's security interests as currently defined by China's leadership are not convergent with those of the United States. China's territorial and jurisdictional disputes are an obvious example. The U.S.'s declared interests are in the peaceful resolution of these disputes, but unfortunately the actions of many of the claimant states do not seem to trend in that direction. If China's confidence in its ability to secure its interests in the South China Sea is growing, it seems likely that we will see more civilian and military maritime activity in the region, more close encounters and an increased likelihood of conflict. China's historical narrative about the importance of its territorial claims make it unlikely that PRC leaders would be able to (or want to) walk back China's claims once it has established greater *de facto* control over these features.

On these issues, a better path for the U.S. is to show China that its own security interests are at cross-purposes. For example, China cannot in the longer run simultaneously maintain stable relations with its neighbors while aggressively pursuing its territorial claims. Nor can it expect other countries in the region and beyond to accept *prima facie* that China's military modernization is not a threat without engaging in greater and more credible transparency about the PLA's capabilities, intentions, and aspirations.

In the longer run, U.S. policy makers need to ask themselves: Which is better for the U.S.—a secure China, or an insecure China? Presumably the answer is a China that is secure about its ability to cooperate on issues where the interests of the two countries converge, and a China that is sure that it *cannot* prevail on issues where they diverge.

Overall, the U.S.-China relationship is going to continue to revolve around a messy and interwoven web of issues. Many of these issues compel the U.S. to cooperate with China out of our own national interest. But there are also issues on which U.S. national interest cannot support Chinese security interests as they are currently constituted. The challenge for U.S. policy makers is to recognize and manage the areas of convergence and divergence.

Mr. SALMON. Thank you.

Given the fact that one of the reasons we moved the hearing today was because they called a 2 o'clock mandatory conference for Republicans, and with my colleagues on the Republican side, I want to give them an opportunity to ask questions before they have to leave, so I am going to start with them.

Mr. DesJarlais, you were here first, so go ahead.

Mr. DESJARLAIS. Thank you, Mr. Chairman.

And I thank the panel for your insightful testimony. It was very helpful and very informative.

Dr. Kaufman, you were kind of wrapping up your testimony regarding the Spratlys and the concerns of Malaysia, Vietnam, Taiwan, Philippines, and others with what they may see as aggression. What would be the consequences for the United States and the region if China were to establish de facto control over the South China Sea?

Ms. KAUFMAN. You always start with the hard questions.

I think the challenge for the U.S. is that other countries in the region are watching to see, of course, what the U.S. will do, regardless of the nature of the U.S.' formal commitment. I mean, in the case of the Philippines, the U.S. has a treaty alliance. I am not an expert on the terms of those, but there is not necessarily an expectation that the U.S. would be involved in an actual conflict. But I think that everyone is waiting to see if the U.S. will back up what it has said is unacceptable in terms of international law and in terms of U.S. policy and partnerships.

And so I tend to think that if the U.S. did nothing, I mean, if China establishes these long-term plans and the U.S. continues to pursue relationships in all of these other domains, that countries in the region will say: Well, you must not really mean it.

I think that everyone understands the very, very difficult military position that the U.S. is in, and people I have talked to in the region are, I think, clear about the fact that this is a very difficult dilemma. I don't think anyone thinks that the U.S. is dying to come in and take care of this problem. So I think they recognize that. But I think that a failure to react on other fronts to instill any kind of pain for doing these things that we said are unacceptable would be a problem for us.

Mr. DESJARLAIS. Thank you.

And I was going to ask a few more questions along that line, but, Dr. Hersh, I heard your comments on TPP. I wanted to get maybe a different perspective.

Dr. Scissors, do you have an opinion in regards to the Trans-Pacific Partnership trade deal that is currently being negotiated, whether it has potential to considerably increase U.S. economic engagement in the region? And would you specifically view this potential deal as an opportunity to promote democratic values in the region?

And, Mr. Han, I will switch to you to answer that after Dr. Scissors' comments.

Mr. SCISSORS. Well, I seem to be constrained more than my fellow panelists because I haven't seen the document, so I don't know what is in it and I don't whether I like it. A lot of the critics of TPP apparently don't care what is in it.

I would love TPP to be a strong free trade agreement. I am an absolute free trader. That is what I want. I don't know what is in it. It is very hard to talk about gains. The studies that are done on TPP make very anodyne, weak, I don't mean weak like wrong, I mean just they have to be very cautious in their assumptions is not very helpful.

I think that if TPP is a strong agreement, which is uncertain, it is a very powerful template for U.S. economic expansion going forward because it will be used as a basis for the TTIP and other agreements. So just looking at the gains from TPP as just the start for the U.S. economy, again, this is if it is a good agreement, I think what we can say as a secondary matter, because I am interested in the economics more than I am in U.S. leadership, is that if we don't move forward with TPP we are reduced to the status of mercenaries in Asia.

What East Asia cares about is economic development. This is the major initiative on the table. We have a number of Asian countries who are already parties. There are others who want to join. If it is no good, we have also blown our economic leadership. If we don't pass it, we have blown our economic leadership. And that leaves us as the people you call when there is a firefight, not the people who come to bring prosperity.

So I can't endorse TPP because I am not allowed to read it yet, but I can endorse the fact that we need a major economic initiative in the region very badly, and I am very hopeful that TPP is that initiative.

Mr. DESJARLAIS. Thank you.

Mr. Han, you can take the reminder of the time.

Mr. HAN. The TPP depends on what is that aiming to. If it is pure economical, I don't have much opinion on that. But if it is about excluding China, there may be another impact or another intention, that will make me doubt whether, one, you can make China as a better international player, economically and politically; second, the Chinese workers and Chinese people will get benefit from this TPP, which my colleague mentioned that it may make Chinese workers' rights better.

And that reminds me of CSR, corporate social responsibility, which has been around for many years. That is much closer to enterprises, and that enterprise is self-policing, but it becomes something else. It never really benefits Chinese workers.

Now, as I said earlier, that workers in China are already taking their fate in their own hands, and Chinese civil society development also is very fast developing. And Chinese people are trying to take everything into our hands and that Chinese Government has to listen to more and more. If TPP is for the purpose of isolating or targetting China, excluding China, then I don't see much benefit Chinese people will have.

Thank you.

Mr. DESJARLAIS. Thank you. Yield back.

Mr. SALMON. Thank you.

Mr. Sherman.

Mr. SHERMAN. Thank you. I do want to chime in on the economic analysis of TPP and TPA.

First, I mean, economists have kind of blinders on. First they look at how TPP will change the status quo. What they don't look at is its number one affect, which is to lock in those portions of the status quo that it locks in.

So if TPP said nothing but there is no change and the United States is locked into the trade policy that has governed us over the last 30 or 40 disastrous years, that would be a huge agreement. If it said nothing but from now on America will never effectively complain about currency manipulation, that is huge.

Now, we have never done it. I mean, we talk about it a little bit or chatter. So the biggest effect of TPP is to lock in a rejection of worrying about focusing and responding to currency manipulation or going the Warren Buffett route of saying, if you want to export to the United States, well, whenever there is an export from the United States, we give the exporter a chit, and if you want to bring something in, you need to buy one of those chits.

So if the agreement did nothing more than lock us into all the bad decisions we have made, it would be bad enough. The other thing the economists don't look at is the rules of origin because, as Dr. Scissors points out, he is not allowed to read the agreement. If you go to the basement, you will see, and I can't reveal exactly what the numbers are here, that goods that are 60 percent made in China, admittedly, which means actually 70, 80, 85 percent made in China, get into the country duty free.

So all the economic analysis is based on what is going to be produced in Japan, what is going to be produced in Vietnam. There is no analysis of what is going to be produced in China and finished in Japan or Vietnam, or slap a ''Made in Vietnam'' sticker on it. So I would be very surprised if it increased our GDP at all.

The next point I want to make is what the Chinese Government lacks is any ideological support for its existence, any source of a mandate from heaven. We survived the Great Depression, as did every other traditional democracy, because even with bad results, we had a system people agreed to.

Now, the divine right of kings works pretty well. People believe it. Democracy has stood the test of time where it has got its root in. Islamic theocracy seems to be able to survive U.S. sanctions more or less. And the Communist religion, when you are truly the vanguard of the proletariat, was sufficient to allow Stalin and Lenin to survive even when there were very bad times for the people of the Soviet Union.

In contrast, this government is not the vanguard of the proletariat. It may be many things, but they are not that. So as long as they deliver tremendous economic growth, what is not to like? But if they face anything like we faced in the 1930s, they have got to retreat to what they are already retreating to, which is nationalism, xenophobia, and you better support us, otherwise China will lose the islets. And there is oil under those islets. And you better believe that because you better believe that you ought to keep us in power.

Mr. Cohen, you mentioned the Philippines is taking China to the international tribunal, and the Chinese are more or less accepting that process?

Mr. COHEN. They are thumbing their nose at it.

Mr. SHERMAN. Okay. I am glad I asked the question.

Also, Mr. Cohen, describe for me how corrupt are the top 2,000 people in the Chinese Government, and when they are corrupt, what do they put their money into? Is it Swiss chateaus, is it Rolex watches? Because if you want to undermine any government anywhere in the world, it is not enough to say they are corrupt. People love the details. The Kardashians, every detail. But at least they are not corrupt. At least they are not governmental. So lifestyles of the rich, famous, and corrupt, what would we see if we could make the TV show?

Mr. COHEN. Well, shall I answer that question, Mr. Chairman?

Mr. SALMON. Yes. In fact, it is your opportunity to answer. You answer however you feel.

Mr. COHEN. I want to first comment on the first point you made, Mr. Sherman, of course, as you know so well, this concern about the TPP and economic relations generally with China involves politics every bit of the way. I have three quick observations on that.

One is we have to recognize our failure to open the IMF, the World Bank, the Asian Development Bank to greater Chinese participation to reflect the new Chinese achievement.

Second, on the TPP, process is as important as substance, and as far as I know, this is a nontransparent process. And I am a citizen, I believe in human rights, and I really am concerned about my inability to know what the TPP really contains. And I realize there are problems in negotiating with 11 other countries if you don't keep things secret, but how do you expect public support for any agreement where the public is being uninformed?

And this is a bad precedent for other governments. Taiwan is in a stalemate now in its cross-strait relations with the mainland because of the fact the people in Taiwan have risen up in the Sunflower Movement, as it was called, against the failure——

Mr. SHERMAN. Mr. Cohen, we do have limited time. If you could focus on the question I asked about corruption.

Mr. COHEN. Well, that was not the only one.

Mr. SHERMAN. It is the only one I asked you to answer, but go ahead.

Mr. COHEN. In any event, on corruption, what we now know after almost 3 years of an intense campaign by the leadership of Mr. Xi Jinping is that there is far more corruption in China than the outer world had realized. And this represents a crisis for them because if he continues to pursue the so-called tigers, like Mr. Zhou Yongkang, who was just dispatched to life imprisonment, and he goes beyond his own enemies like Zhou Yongkang to, in an objective fashion, pursue other leaders in China, this can lead to the destruction of the party.

On the other hand, if he doesn't pursue these people, it is going to lose public support. And leaders before him, and he also has agreed, failure to pursue corruption is a life-or-death question for the party. They may get through the next 8 years of his term, but it is not going to go far beyond that.

So I think you put your finger on a critical issue, and the problem is for us what to do. Right now China is asking us to find and return to China people the Government of China is pursuing as being corrupt elements. And the U.S., not having an extradition treaty with China because we can't send people back to a legal system we don't trust, doesn't know what to do. We were going to have the head of the Chinese anticorruption campaign visit Washington at this time, but because of inability to make an agreement on how we are going to handle their demands to send back as many as 150 leading people, he is not coming.

The other problem is, what is corruption? Much of what passes for corruption in the eyes of the Chinese people may not be direct bribery, but it is the use of Guanxi, relationships. If I am the son of a leading member of the Communist Party, everybody knows that when I try to make a deal, and it offers so many opportunities. And they have gone into every kind of business. It isn't just they spend the money on luxury things. They are making hundreds of millions of dollars.

And one problem is what can you do about family networks—Xi Jinping himself has this problem in his own family. He has got people who have made lots of money by using their access to the top. So this is a huge problem for China. It may be a life-or-death struggle.

Mr. SHERMAN. Thank you.

We are debating whether to withdraw from the Middle East all military force right now on the floor, so I am going to have to go to the floor. I yield back.

Mr. SALMON. Thank you, Mr. Chairman.

I am going to yield to Mr. Perry.

Mr. PERRY. Thank you, Mr. Chairman.

And as my good friend from Sherman Oaks is leaving the room, I must say that I found it curious that the statement that China, as being the vanguard of the proletariat, would be concerned in times of peril in keeping their power and they would say to their citizens, ''Well, you must be with us because there is oil under those islands,'' it seems to me, in my lifetime, they said, ''You must be with us or you end up in jail.'' And that is what works, and that is what will work in the future if there are times of peril.

But that having been said, I came here thinking that we would talk about aircraft carriers and increased economic activity such that the West and the United States in particular would find it problematic and itself behind.

But looking at some of the statistics here, you look at GDP, and, Dr. Scissors, with all due respect, at least some of these numbers, from 10.4 in 2010 to 7.4 in 2014, and looking at in the next 6 years down to 5.9, looking at birthrates from 5.8 per woman in 1964 to 1.6 in 2012, and then looking at the labor force shrinking by one-fifth over the next 50 years, I thought maybe we would discuss like we believe in—well, a lot of us, there are a lot that don't—but there are a lot of us that believe in capitalism in the United States and that this is free democracy and free trade and capitalism has done well for the West and our system is the best and it has lasted and endured the longest of the longest of modern governments because of that, and we have always kind of eschewed Communism as a moribund program that simply can't work over the long haul.

And with those statistics and with the concern in America today of a rising China and so on and so forth, I would actually like to ask you, Dr. Scissors and Mr. Cohen, in particular, what you think, like how long do we have to wait? If we believe that what we have is right and what they have is wrong and cannot endure, are we close to the end? Is the end 50 years away? Ten years? When will it collapse under its own weight? When will it pull the Soviet Union and unexpectedly, as you said, we won't be ready? Is there something on the horizon that some people see and some people don't?

Mr. SCISSORS. As I said in my opening remarks, I know the timing of the hearing messed a few things up, I am a stagnation guy, not a collapse guy. The mixed economy that China has doesn't lend itself to acute economic crises. Some of my colleagues are experts on politics. I am not. But some of the statistics you cited, for people who believe in GDP, first of all, I think the party is exaggerating their GDP growth, but even then, it is on a straight line down, the growth. Aging, debt, all of it says stagnation.

And we have seen that countries can stay stuck for a long time without instability. None of them are middle-income countries run by the Communist Party. North Korea is just poor. It is kind of more remarkable that they have had not very much instability there.

But I think in terms of the challenge to the United States, the challenge to competitive market capitalism when we practice it properly, that challenge is already going away. The Chinese model is already fading. I was sitting in front of the Congress in 2009 when people were panicked that China was going to take over the world, and I think that panic has receded considerably and it is going to continue to recede.

So I don't know enough about Chinese politics to say, "Hey, I think the economic stagnation is going to breed a collapse." It is possible. Ranking Member Sherman just said, my colleagues have said, the party has survived on delivering the goods economically and they are not going to be able to unless they change course.

But what I can say is, to echo Professor Cohen, I think China has peaked economically. And the economic challenge to the United States is not going to go away, China is not suddenly going to become small, but the fear that we have had of China overtaking us, eclipsing the way we do things, that in my view is already gone, and if it isn't already gone, it will be gone for almost everyone in a few years.

Mr. PERRY. Dr. Cohen, quickly.

And if I get time, Dr. Hersh, I would like to hear your comments as well.

Mr. HERSH. We began engaging China post-1989 Tiananmen massacre with the idea that commerce would lead to political changes of a more evolutionary basis, and that happened here in Washington. We had our own version of the Long March to get China permanent normal trade relations and then to get China into the WTO. China has certainly integrated itself into the global trade and investment system over this time, but I don't think we have seen the political changes that we thought would flow from these economic changes and more integration with the ideas and technologies of the outside world.

Has this created pressures for political change? Maybe, but not necessarily in the ways that we had expected. Those who are successful in the new China, in China, Inc. are greatly supportive of the way that the government has prosecuted its policymaking and secured its position and power. But this growth and transformation has also unleashed the most rapid increase in inequality almost that the world has ever experienced, and this is creating real risk for social and political instability that I don't think we have good forecasts for how those might disrupt China's political system.

There is clearly quite a bit of economic gain to be had from economic integration with China, as well as other partners in the region, but who benefits from that, how the gains are to be distributed depends entirely on the kinds of rules that we set in these international agreements.

Mr. COHEN. I could answer just a little bit.

Mr. SALMON. Time from the gentleman has expired. We probably need to get to the next questioner, Mr. Rohrabacher.

Mr. ROHRABACHER. Yes, thank you.

Well, I have sat through these sessions where people are predicting that if we do certain things economically for China that that would result in the type of political reform then and reform toward making a country less antagonistic and more benevolent than they would be otherwise.

We have now had about 20 years to see if that theory works, and I think that it has been a resounding failure, all the things that were promised us if we just bolster the economic situation of China by permitting a trade agreement, which obviously has enriched and empowered that China. Do they have free labor unions now? No. Do they have opposition parties? No. Does China today have fewer territorial claims and is less provocative toward their neighbors? No. I just heard all of these predictions, and they turned out to be not true.

Now, I know that Mr. Cohen has suggested that you have to give the Chinese Communist Party credit, at least look at what they have done. No. No. The fact is that the Chinese people could well have been living better today had we not had a Communist Chinese dictatorship over them and bolstered it a number of years ago. I think they didn't have the same kind of dictatorship in other countries that had Chinese-type of backgrounds, and those people prospered and yet have freedom at the same time, or at least a greater degree of freedom than you have in the mainland of China.

So let me suggest that when we are talking about the TPP, we hear some of the same rhetoric about the TPP, how it is going to bring this prosperity and better trained jobs, and I think that all the farmers in America thought that we would be feeding China, and now China is a massive food exporter to the United States and putting some of our people out of work.

And by the way, when you talk about the TPP, at least with most-favored-nation status, we pretty well knew what exactly that meant. People keep using phrases like "free trade" with the TPP. How do we know it is free trade? We don't even know if it is free trade at all. Even with MFN or WTO it wasn't free trade with China. With China, we ended up with, of course, letting them in most-favored-nation status and into the WTO.

We basically have a clique that is able to manipulate the trade now and has enriched the clique. But as Mr. Han was suggesting, there are a lot of people left out of the clique and they don't have any economic rights at all.

So I would just like to leave it with this. And maybe, we have got about 1½ minutes now, if you have to bet on which change, what is going to happen? This fellow over here is a stagnation guy instead of a collapse guy. What about the rest of you? Are you collapse guys or stagnation guys? And I would just like to hear that simple answer from all of you here, Mr. Han first, then Mr. Cohen, and right on down. Are you a collapse guy or a stagnation guy? Are they going to collapse and then the democrats are going to take over and have a democratic free society or is it going to stagnate?

Mr. HAN. I would like to say it is a process. It is not a flip of the hand thing. It is a process. As I said earlier in my talk, workers without freedom of association, we are getting rights to collective bargaining. And now collective bargaining, this idea, is being accepted more and more.

Mr. ROHRABACHER. I agree with you that it is a process, and that means that a process, as we determine what will happen and what the process will be, we will determine whether or not a Communist, strong Communist Party that threatens the rest of the world still continues in power. We will determine it, because it is a process, that we will impact as we impacted it with MFN and WTO in a way that strengthened the hand of the despots.

Mr. Cohen, are you a stagnation guy or a collapse guy?

Mr. COHEN. Right now I think the Chinese Government is threatened with Brezhnev kind of administration of the economy that ultimately led to collapse in the Soviet Union, but we shouldn't underestimate the imagination and dynamism of the Chinese leaders in meeting some of these international economic problems. The AIIB and related institutions are an example of their giving an imaginative response that put the U.S. Government back on its heels with surprise.

So I think I agree with Mr. Han that the current situation is a struggle, it is up for grabs. And I think I agree with you, Mr. Rohrabacher, about what we do can have a profound influence.

But I do want to point out, apropos of what you said earlier, that the Chiang Kai-shek regime in Taiwan was as harsh a military dictatorship as we see now on the mainland. The Park Chung-hee administration in South Korea was similar. I opposed both of them very actively. But the fact is, as an objective observer, I have to say that for a certain period, as a government gets going, dictatorship seems to enable economic progress, but that very economic progress leads to the kind of ferment that we are beginning to witness in China. And what the outcome of that ferment will be is really in part up to us, mostly up to the Chinese people.

Mr. ROHRABACHER. And the difference, of course, is those two dictatorships did not pose an ever-enlarging threat to their neighbors and to the peace of the world. Chiang Kai-shek didn't threaten, I don't think, he didn't threaten anybody, and after he got to Taiwan—well, we could go into that—and neither did South Korea.

China poses a huge threat. The building of these islands and then making greater declarations of ownership of territorial rights, if there is anything that is a threat to the peace of the world, and our administration hasn't said anything about that. By the way,

Putin occupies a given small, tiny area of Ukraine because it is made up of pro-Russian people and he has gone there protecting those pro-Russian people. Shouldn't have done it, but you hear this is a monstrous invasion. China makes claims of 100 times more territory than that, that would cut Japan and Korea off from their trading routes, and you don't hear anybody complaining about that.

Better go on to the last time. Collapse or are we going to stagnation?

Mr. HERSH. I don't know if I would go to stagnation, but definitely a slowdown. The organic forces in China's economy that have led to such rapid growth to this point, those are not going to continue, although China will continue to grow at a healthy pace. Where China's economy is already coequal in size to the United States, that means it is going to continue to pull away from——

Mr. ROHRABACHER. Unless, of course, we are so stupid that we keep bolstering this same dictatorial government that threatens the word.

Dr. Kaufman.

Ms. KAUFMAN. I think that historically we have not seen very many successful democratic transitions that haven't taken place either as a result of leadership decisions or war. I think that many people in China were paying a lot of attention to what happened in 2011, and I don't think that they find the outcome of the Arab Spring very appealing. I think that a lot of people are pretty unhappy with certain aspects of the CCP, but I don't think that many people see very many viable alternatives.

Mr. ROHRABACHER. Okay. One last thought, Mr. Chairman. That is, we had a turning point in the history of the world, and there were two of them in close proximity. One was the collapse of the Soviet Union. I am proud to have been part of Ronald Reagan's team in the White House for 7½ years with him, served as special assistant, and did everything we could to bring down the Soviet Union. And it came down in a peaceful way without having direct fights between Soviet troops and American troops. What a great accomplishment that was.

We could have had the same type of accomplishment in China, but Reagan was no longer President. Herbert Walker Bush was President. And at Tiananmen Square, it is my belief, Mr. Chairman, had Ronald Reagan been President, he would have picked up the phone, as his intelligence officer said, they are about to unleash the army on Tiananmen Square, and Reagan would have said: If you want unleash the army on Tiananmen Square, no more open markets, no more investment, no more credits, all the deals are off. And they wouldn't have put the army in and we would have a democratic China today that wasn't threatening the peace of the world.

Yes, it is a process, and we need to play our part.

Thank you very much.

Mr. SALMON. Thank you.

Save myself for last.

I, as a young man, did a mission for the Mormon Church in Taiwan and spent 2 years there, during the time when Chiang Ching-kuo, Chiang Kai-shek's son, was the President, and there was no freedom of speech, there was no right to assemble, and there was really no freedom of the press per se. And so I lived that up close and personal. I was there in 1979 when Jimmy Carter severed diplomatic ties with Taiwan, normalized relations with China. And at that time we clearly advocated a one-China policy, and we have done that ever since.

Things have changed now. Taiwan is not anymore an autocratic, authoritarian regime. It is now a thriving democracy. And a lot of the policies that we have toward Taiwan right now seem to be kind of outdated.

And I am just wondering, I know, Mr. Cohen, you have been a strong advocate, as I have in the past, on the one-China policy, but we have seen how the one-China policy really works with Hong Kong, where they said it was going to be one China, two systems, and that is a joke. It is a real joke, because they don't even have the ability to choose their own Chief Executive. That is delivered to them from Beijing. You get to pick, but you get to pick from the candidates that we choose. There is no universal suffrage, not really, not in Hong Kong.

And the people on Taiwan, they have watched that. And as they think about a peaceful reunification one day and they see how Hong Kong is treated, they are thinking, ''Not on your life, we don't want to go under those kind of circumstances, we have a thriving democracy that works.''

And then I see how Taiwan tries to do a magnanimous gesture during the Ebola outbreak and they offer their support to the World Health Organization, and what happens? Politics, lousy, stupid politics.

Same thing with their ability to be able to join the all-hands-on-deck call for fighting terrorism globally. They can't participate in Interpol. In fact, I dropped a bill just recently and it was marked up in the full committee on Foreign Affairs that says that they should have observer status in Interpol. Why not? I mean, it is ludicrous.

Some of the walking on egg shells that we do to try to appease China on this one-China policy thing seems to be really unsustainable, and I am wondering, is it time for us to look at maybe tweaking that a little bit.

Mr. Cohen, what are your thoughts?

Mr. COHEN. The time is coming, because next year, as you know, President Ma steps down. No matter who replaces him, and it is likely to be the DPP candidate, this is going to create a new kind of difficulty in cross-strait relations. We have had a pretty good ride the last 7 years because Ma has made so many agreements without prejudicing the security of Taiwan. But he has reached the limit, and the people of Taiwan, as you know, are expressing they want to have more say in Taiwan's future.

Mr. SALMON. Tired of it.

Mr. COHEN. China may be getting more nationalistic and less patient. So I am afraid you are going to have to give this more attention over the next few years, because there is going to be a return of tension over Taiwan that may make the South China Sea look like less of a threat in comparison.

Mr. SALMON. Well, Mr. Cohen, I remember vividly when Lee Teng-hui was being sworn in as the first freely elected President of Taiwan, Beijing responded by lobbing missiles into the Taiwan Strait. Now, while we had a policy of strategic ambiguity, which was the policy we have kind of articulated for decades, President Clinton kind of erased some of that ambiguity by sending the Nimitz down the Taiwan Strait to give a little bit of clarity. And what happened was we deescalated the tensions in the region.

But I am just not sure right now that this administration is even up to that, of giving any kind of clarity on what exactly we are going to do to uphold the Taiwan Relations Act.

Dr. Scissors, do you have a comment?

Mr. SCISSORS. This is a very quick, and it is intentionally cheeky, but it is also real. If you finish the TPP and you let Taiwan join before China, you have done something to change your recognition of the two countries.

Mr. SALMON. Right. And honestly, Dr. Scissors, there is a lot of dialogue. We did a delegation over to China, Taiwan, Japan just a couple of years ago, and then we did another meeting about 3 months ago with Ed Royce, and the topic of Taiwan coming in the second round of TPP came up. There was support across the board, from both Republicans and Democrats. I think if you polled Members across the board in the Congress, you would find far more support for Taiwan coming into the TPP ahead of mainland China. I think you would find that support very robust.

Mr. SCISSORS. Right.

Mr. SALMON. Some of these international bodies, I think, really need to have the input that Taiwan has, and we could probably do that without jeopardizing our sacred one-China policy. But is there a way for us to maybe tweak that a little bit?

Mr. COHEN. I have been urging Taiwan to do more on its own. For example, Taiwan, as you know, occupies the biggest island in the Spratlys. I think, since President Ma is an expert in public international law and is about to retire from office, he ought to lead an effort to come up with imaginative proposals beyond the general language he has already given us on May 25 that would encourage a settlement of these issues. We need imagination.

Taiwan should make its way back by becoming a host to the other contending nations and turning Itu Aba of a conference center, a negotiation, a workshop dialogue center that will promote, I think, the kinds of solutions that people aren't putting forth now. People are just talking about strengthening their militaries. And while that is useful and necessary, we have got to do a lot more. We have to have more imaginative solutions.

And here is a way for Taiwan to help, just the way they managed to make a fisheries agreement with Japan in the East China See. Imaginative, vigorous diplomacy on Taiwan's part, in addition to our support, I think would be very important.

Mr. SALMON. Thank you, Mr. Cohen.

Mr. Han, we had a great meeting with several of the business leaders, as well as some of the, I think, Hong Kong greats. We met with Martin Lee, we met with Anson Chan when I was there. And it was coincidental because I was there for the 1997 handover ceremony and I met with Martin Lee back then, so it kind of felt like deja vu a little bit, or as a great baseball player once said, deja vu all over again.

But do you think that the opportunity for suffrage, universal suffrage in Hong Kong, will come to fruition in your lifetime?

Mr. HAN. Not only Hong Kong, but China as well, I believe so. But the real opportunity and the hope is the changing of mainland China. Hong Kong cannot get full democracy without China becoming democracy. That is not possible. So I count on China.

And I agree with Mr. Rohrabacher, who said China did not answer to the international community for nearly anything. And China, to my understanding about this government, they will not answer positively to military responses. But one thing I am sure I already see that myself experiencing this: Chinese Government is already answering to its own people, although it is not full. For example, they arrest lawyers, they arrest journalists, but they are answering to hundreds of millions of workers' demands to the right to collective bargaining, and the next one will be naturally, slowly develop into freedom of association, a union, maybe not purely freedom of association, but with a solely collective bargaining-oriented trade union.

So if Chinese Government can answer and will answer to 100 million of Chinese workers, I do believe, even if they don't answer to the U.S. military, but they will have to become more and more democratic.

Mr. SALMON. Well, I thank you. This has been a very invigorating conversation. I appreciate all the patience on the part of the witnesses today for the time changes. I apologize for doing that to you, but we just thought it was so important to get this done, especially because Mr. Han is not here all the time. So we wanted to make sure that we got it done today, so it necessitated us moving the time. So thank you very much and thank you so much for your patience.

This committee is adjourned.

[Whereupon, at 2:47 p.m., the subcommittee was adjourned.]

APPENDIX

Material Submitted for the Record

SUBCOMMITTEE HEARING NOTICE
COMMITTEE ON FOREIGN AFFAIRS
U.S. HOUSE OF REPRESENTATIVES
WASHINGTON, DC 20515-6128

Subcommittee on Asia and the Pacific
Matt Salmon (R-AZ), Chairman

June 17, 2015

TO: MEMBERS OF THE COMMITTEE ON FOREIGN AFFAIRS

You are respectfully requested to attend an OPEN hearing of the Committee on Foreign Affairs, to be held by the Subcommittee on Asia and the Pacific in Room 2255 of the Rayburn House Office Building (and available live on the Committee website at http://www.ForeignAffairs.house.gov):

DATE: Wednesday, June 17, 2015

TIME: 1:00 p.m.

SUBJECT: China's Rise: The Strategic Impact of Its Economic and Military Growth

WITNESSES: Derek M. Scissors, Ph.D.
                 Resident Scholar
                 American Enterprise Institute

                 Alison Kaufman, Ph.D.
                 Senior Research Scientist
                 China Studies Division
                 CNA Corporation

                 Mr. Jerome A. Cohen
                 Professor and Co-Director
                 U.S.-Asia Law Institute
                 New York University School of Law

                 Mr. Han Dongfang
                 Founder and Director
                 China Labour Bulletin

                 Adam Hersh, Ph.D.
                 Senior Economist
                 Roosevelt Institute

By Direction of the Chairman

The Committee on Foreign Affairs seeks to make its facilities accessible to persons with disabilities. If you are in need of special accommodations, please call 202/225-5021 at least four business days in advance of the event, whenever practicable. Questions with regard to special accommodations in general (including availability of Committee materials in alternative formats and assistive listening devices) may be directed to the Committee.

COMMITTEE ON FOREIGN AFFAIRS

MINUTES OF SUBCOMMITTEE ON _____*Asia and the Pacific*_____ HEARING

Day___*Wednesday*___Date_____*6/17/15*_____Room_____*2255*_____

Starting Time _____*1:06pm*_____Ending Time _____*2:46pm*_____

Recesses |___| (____to ____) (____to ____) (____to ____) (____to ____) (____to ____) (____to ____)

Presiding Member(s)

Matt Salmon

Check all of the following that apply:

Open Session ☑
Executive (closed) Session ☐
Televised ☐

Electronically Recorded (taped) ☐
Stenographic Record ☐

TITLE OF HEARING:

China's Rise: The Strategic Impact of its Economic and Military Growth

SUBCOMMITTEE MEMBERS PRESENT:

Jeff Duncan, Scott DesJarlais, Scott Perry, Dana Rohrabacher, Brad Sherman

NON-SUBCOMMITTEE MEMBERS PRESENT: *(Mark with an * if they are not members of full committee.)*

HEARING WITNESSES: Same as meeting notice attached? Yes ☑ No ☐
(If "no", please list below and include title, agency, department, or organization.)

STATEMENTS FOR THE RECORD: *(List any statements submitted for the record.)*

TIME SCHEDULED TO RECONVENE _____
or
TIME ADJOURNED _____*2:46*_____

Subcommittee Staff Director